V. N. TATISHCHEV
GUARDIAN OF THE
PETRINE REVOLUTION

RUDOLPH L. DANIELS

FRANKLIN PUBLISHING COMPANY

Philadelphia

Preface

In spite of his importance in Russian history, only two full-length biographies of V. N. Tatishchev have been published. In the middle of the nineteenth century, N. A. Popov wrote his *V. N. Tatishchev and His Time*, and in the 1950's Conrad Grau published *Der Wirtschafts-organisater, Staatsmann, und Wissenschaftler Vasilij N. Tatiscev*. Both works, however, appeared before the discovery of certain important sources, and fail to place Tatishchev into proper historical perspective by describing his activities and writings in separate chapters rather than in the biographical framework. *V. N. Tatishchev: Guardian of the Petrine Revolution* includes his intellectual and political achievements in the biography proper as well as presenting a comprehensive view of Tatishchev as an historian. Such an organization will provide the reader with a greater insight into the development of Tatishchev as a government official, and, at the same time, affords a clearer picture of the problems confronting the lower nobility in Russia in the period following the reign of Peter the Great.

For the reader's convenience I have translated all Russian book titles in the text into English and have used the Library of Congress system of transliteration throughout.

I am most grateful to Dr. Edward C. Thaden of the University of Illinois at Chicago Circle whose assistance and encouragement I have enjoyed throughout the preparation of this book and my entire graduate career. I would also like to thank Dr. S. V. Utechin of the Pennsylvania State University for his many suggestions and encouragement. Needless to say, there are many others who have offered suggestions and criticisms. I thank all of them.

R. L. DANIELS
Dubuque, Iowa 1972

The author acknowledges with appreciation the permission of the publishers of the Slavonic Review (London) to include in this volume portions of an article, "V. N. Tatishchev and the Succession Crisis of 1730," which appeared in Vol. XLIX, No. 117, October 1971.

CONTENTS

V. N. TATISHCHEV
GUARDIAN OF THE
PETRINE REVOLUTION

Chapter I

Introduction

Born in the latter half of the seventeenth century, V. N. Tatishchev lived through one of the most turbulent periods in Russian history. Son of a nobleman, he served in the newly created civil administration and personally took part in many of the Petrine innovations. Even more important, after Peter the Great's death, Tatishchev witnessed the retardation of the pace of reform and the nobility's adjustment to its new service obligations. Hence, Tatishchev personally experienced the transformation of the Russian nobility and the growth of a new mentality created by the Petrine civil service.

During his reign Peter the Great tried to transform Russia into a modern, western state.[1] In doing so he revolutionized almost every aspect of Muscovite life to make it conform to his ideal of a Russian Empire. With a close group of reformers, he accomplished a great deal of his task in spite of opposition from traditionally minded elements of Russian society. By the end of his reign in 1725, Peter modernized, to a large degree, Russian commerce and industry, the Orthodox Church, and government administration, and required the Russian nobility to adopt Western European customs and culture.

Peter wanted Russian industry to become self-sufficient and to provide for him the materials needed for war. He personally sought Western craftsmen to employ them in Russian trades and industries. Although he concentrated on heavy industry, Peter encouraged trade, and at the same time decreed a tariff to encourage domestic manufacturing. He also designed his new capital, St. Petersburg, as the commercial center for his Empire.

Such venerable institutions as the Orthodox Church were not sacrosanct to Peter's modernization policy.[2] In 1721, under the direction of the Archbishop of Novgorod, Theofan Prokopovich, Peter abolished the Patriarchate and established the Holy Synod. The Holy Synod, officiated by a layman, functioned as a college or a committee to administer Church affairs. Besides bringing the Church administration in tune with his overall policies, Peter acquired Church lands which had hitherto remained out of reach of the State.

1

The core of the Petrine reforms was the first Emperor's centralizing of government administration. In 1711, Peter created a Senate to promulgate his decrees and to devise methods to carry them out. Six years later he replaced the overlapping Muscovite administrative offices, the *prikazi*, with nine colleges. Peter thereby departmentalized government administration for the entire Empire into bureaucracies for: Foreign Relations, State Revenue, Expenditure, Control, Justice, Army, Admirality, Commerce, and Mines and Manufactures.

The collegial administrative system had a great effect on Russian society inasmuch as Peter needed personnel to fill the positions in his newly created civil service. The formation of the civil service made new demands, particularly on the Russian nobility.[3] Previously, the Russian nobleman had served the Tsar in the military for limited periods of time for land allotments. The nobleman's rank and function in the military were determined by an elaborate and complex system called the *mestnichestvo*, according to which members of a noble's family had to be appointed to an equal or higher position than that held by his ancestors. The system was cumbersome and often brought about quarrels among the noblemen. The *mestnichestvo* was abolished in 1689, since by that time it only hampered military efficiency.

The long service tradition of the nobility made it natural for Peter the Great to look to them to furnish personnel for his civil service. In contrast to his limited term of military service, the nobleman was now compelled to remain permanently in administrative positions. No longer receiving land allotments for service, he became a salaried official and was expected to develop particular skills and serve efficiently. In place of the *mestnichestvo*, Peter created an orderly Table of Ranks. Each rank denoted a person's function and responsibility in State service. Theoretically, at least, anyone and everyone entered the civil service at the lowest of 14 ranks. Upon reaching the eighth, an official acquired the status of hereditary nobility for his family.

Peter the Great's civil service and Table of Ranks actually transformed the old nobility into a new class. Peter forced the nobleman to serve within the framework of an impersonal bureaucracy that no longer permitted him to stand in a direct and personal relationship to the Tsar. Perhaps just as important, a commoner could now hold a higher position in the civil service than did many noblemen, and could acquire the status of nobility by reaching the eighth rank. To a large degree, Peter changed the concept of nobility, and systematically forced the Russian nobleman into greater subservience to the State, often making him feel that he had lost his dignity and social position.

In the years immediately following the Petrine reforms, members of the nobility and their sons adjusted to their new situation. At first, they tried to slow down the pace of reform and to limit Peter's service requirements to their own advantage. By the middle of the eighteenth century, however, Russian noblemen realized that they could preserve their dignity and social position within the Petrine formula. Moreover, now that both the military and civil service demanded that he learn skills and techniques imported from western Europe, the nobleman quickly saw himself as part of an elite that possessed this desired expertise. He came to identify himself with the task of bringing western European culture and technology to Russia; i.e., he became a *Kulturträger*. Within a few decades after Peter the Great's reign, noblemen accepted their service obligations as a matter of course.

Most accounts of Russian history skim over the period immediately following the reign of Peter the Great. Rather than describing the development of the new service nobility and the efforts made to preserve the Petrine reforms, they trace the rapid succession of monarchs and the influence of foreigners and intriguers who used high government offices for personal gains. Nevertheless, the Russian Empire grew culturally and economically according to the Petrine design. It is highly improbable, therefore, that the major achievements of Peter the Great could have survived over a generation of such apparent misrule without a number of significant individuals who desired to continue the work of reform. V. N. Tatishchev was one of these individuals.

V. N. Tatishchev was no ordinary civil official, and an account of his activities is particularly significant for an understanding of the transformation of the Russian nobility and the political, cultural, and intellectual growth of Russia in the period following Peter the Great's reign. Because of his education and experience gained during the Petrine era, Tatishchev was in the forefront of Russian political and intellectual life in the second quarter of the eighteenth century. During the succession crisis of 1730, he submitted a project for a general reform of state administration. He was also active in the Urals factory administration, and headed the Orenburg and Kalmyk Commissions along the Empire's frontier.

Tatishchev's writings are of particular importance in understanding the new mentality created by the Petrine civil service. In 1733, he wrote a "Conversation of Two Friends on the Use of Knowledge and Education,"[4] in which he addressed himself to some of the problems which Russia faced in the second quarter of the eighteenth century. In 1740, he again discussed at greater length in his *Testament*[5] the nobil-

3

ity's situation in the wake of the Petrine reforms. As an outgrowth of his administrative tasks, Tatishchev compiled a *Geographical Lexicon*[6] in which he attempted to identify the major physical features of the Russian Empire. He also wrote the first scientific survey of early Russian history. More than a multi-volume compilation of historical information, Tatishchev's *Russian History*[7] reflects his attitude as a State administrator in the decades following the Petrine reforms. Above all, V. N. Tatishchev dedicated his life's work to bring into realization Peter the Great's ideal of a Russian Empire.

Chapter II

First Years in State Service

Tatishchev's first years in State service provided him with knowledge and experience for his future tasks as administrator and historian. From 1704 until 1719, he served in various capacities and had frequent contact with Peter the Great. Later, he was placed in charge of the State metal factory system in the Ural Mountains. During this period, he developed a particular outlook toward the State and State service which he retained throughout his life.

Vasilii Nikitich Tatishchev was born on 19 April 1686 in or near the city of Pskov.[1] His family was related to the line of Smolensk princes who, according to tradition, traced their ancestry back to Riurik, the reputed founder of the Russian monarchy. One Vasilii Iurievitch received the surname Tatishchev, meaning "seeker of evil doers," as a reward for having discovered a plot against Grand Prince Vasilii Dmitrievich of Moscow. Nikita Alekseevich Tatishchev, Vasilii Nikitich's father, moved the family from Smolensk to Pskov, where he served as *voevoda*.[2]

Little is known about V. N. Tatishchev's formative years. It is known, however, that a distant family relationship with Praskovia Saltykova, wife of Tsar Ivan V, provided young Vasilii and his brother Ivan with access to the royal court.[3] It seems that the Tatishchev brothers visited the royal family quite often, and, in all likelihood, they became acquainted with Peter the Great at that time. As for his education, all that is known is that his father assumed personal charge of his upbringing.

In his *Testament*, Tatishchev wrote that he and his brother Ivan Nikitich entered State service in 1704.[4] Two years later, Peter the Great assigned the brothers to join a new army regiment which was being formed by A. I. Ivanov.[5] In August of the same year, the regiment left Moscow with V. N. Tatishchev, age 20, commissioned lieutenant. In 1707, the regiment was named the Azov Dragoons and was ordered to join other troops under the commond of B. P. Sheremetev near Smolensk. Tatishchev experienced battle with the Dragoons in June of 1709. Later, on the 21st, they participated in the Battle of Poltava, which was a decisive conflict in the Great Northern War.

In 1710, when the Azov Dragoons were located in southwest Russia, Tatishchev led 300 down the Pripet River from Pinsk to Kiev.[6] During the journey, Tatishchev stopped near the village of Korosten to visit a grave which the local inhabitants believed to be that of Prince Igor.[7] In 1711, he took part in the unsuccessful Pruth Campaign, during which he formed a close and lasting friendship with Archbishop Theofan Prokopovich, who was at that time Rector of the Theological Academy at Kiev.[8] Although Tatishchev was relieved of regimental duty shortly thereafter, he remained in the Azov region until he journeyed abroad.

In 1712, Tatishchev was sent to western Europe to study artillery and engineering and to observe the armies of other nations.[9] He remained in Berlin for some time and frequented the Royal Library and the Academy of the King of Prussia. It is highly probable that he then met Johann Leonhard Frisch, who was considered an expert on Slavic languages and cultures.[10] Tatishchev also traveled to Dresden and Breslau, but no information exists about his activities in those cities.

In the winter of 1714, he visited his former commander, Sheremetev, who was then stationed in Lublin.[11] During his stay in Lublin, he heard that an old woman who lived in the area had been condemned to death for witchcraft. Not believing in sorcery, Tatishchev tried to convince his former commander not to listen to the rumors and to spare the woman's life. Sheremetev refused to do so, but he did grant Tatishchev permission to speak with her. During their conversation, Tatishchev asked the woman to perform three acts of sorcery, which she could not do. When Sheremetev saw this, he revoked the death sentence and had her sent to a convent instead. This incident, if nothing else, reveals that Tatishchev was far ahead of his contemporaries in his views on sorcery. In May, he left Sheremetev to resume his studies.[12]

Artillery and engineering did not occupy all of Tatishchev's study time abroad. During those four year, he purchased books on history, geography, and a French grammar.[13] Moreover, as he himself stated, he perfected his knowledge of German and Polish.[14]

When he returned to Russia in 1716, he registered at the Moscow Artillery School to study under Field Marshal Jacob Bruce.[15] An intimate of Peter the Great, Bruce was then regarded as the foremost artillery expert in Russia.[16] Although he had been born in Moscow of foreign parentage, he studied mathematics and engineering in England, France, and Holland. In May 1716, Bruce appointed Tatishchev lieutenant of the first artillery regiment and increased his salary to 12 rubles a month.[17] Later, at the request of Peter the Great, Tatishchev worked

6

under Bruce's direction to draw up a plan for defense of military fortresses. In January 1717, he directed the construction of the armory in the new capital, St. Petersburg.

By that spring, both Field Marshal Bruce and Peter the Great thought enough of Tatishchev's abilities to give him his first important assignments. For his first task, Bruce sent him to Germany to work on artillery and the administration of military supplies. His second assignment was to take charge of the tribute which Peter collected from the cities conquered during the war with Sweden. On his way to Germany, Tatishchev first stopped at Memel to inspect the unloading of war supplies.[18] From mid-May until the end of June, he took charge of cannon casting and the distribution of material for Prince A. I. Repnin's division in Danzig. He then went to Torun until the end of July to direct artillery repairs. There can be no doubt of the success of Tatishchev's first assignment. In a letter to Bruce, Prince Repnin wrote, "Tatishchev is a good man, he fulfilled his task in my division extraordinarily well. Until now it has not been."[19] At Torun, his workers titled him "master craftsman."

In his *Russian History,* Tatishchev described an incident which occurred during his stay in Poland.[20] During a dinner conversation, Peter the Great and his friends were discussing the adventures and accomplishments of his father, Tsar Alexis. At one point, Count Musin-Pushkin, whom Tatishchev described as "full of deceit and hypocrisy," belittled Alexis' deeds by saying that his reign was successful only because he had appointed good advisors such as Morozov. Peter suddenly leaped to his feet. He angrily called Musin-Pushkin a hypocrite for praising his reign by degrading that of his father. Peter then turned to Prince Iakov Dolgorukii and asked him to judge the two rules. He told Dolgorukii that, although he too was annoying sometimes beyond toleration, "I see that you really love me and the State and speak the truth [and] for that I thank you from my innermost."[21]

Dolgorukii first asked Peter to sit down while he considered the problem and, as Tatishchev noted, thought what they "wanted to hear." After some time, he began by saying that Peter had three tasks during his reign, the first of which concerned internal affairs, particularly jurisprudence. Here, Dolgurukii thought, Tsar Alexis accomplished more, because he was freer to do so. At the same time, he said that Peter could excel his father once the war with Sweden ended. Peter's second task was to organize the army. Although Tsar Alexis established a good army, Peter built it anew and won a strong position for Russia in the affairs of Europe. However, Dolgorukii cautioned, the real

7

answer to which sovereign accomplished more in this second task would be determined by the outcome of the war. Peter's third task was to build a fleet. There can be no doubt, he said, that Peter built the navy and gained esteem for himself and for Russia among all nations.

Following the comparison, Dolgorukii answered Musin-Pushkin by observing that all monarchs have advisors. It is the wise monarch who chooses intelligent and loyal counselors and who can judge the worth and truth of their advice.

Peter listened patiently to Dolgorukii's comments. Then he rose from his chair and kissed the prince, calling him his "loyal slave." He said that in few had he found such loyalty.[22]

The event obviously made a strong impression on Tatishchev—strong enough to include it in his *History* many years later. Peter did not want Musin-Pushkin's bootlicking. If Dolgorukii praised him, it was in a different way. He pointed out Peter's accomplishments without fawning, and he evaluated them according to the growth and modernization of the Russian State. Tatishchev was aware of Dolgorukii's "loyalty," and he took the lesson to heart. It seems that, when Peter was in Danzig in 1716, he heard a rumor that an ikon of the Last Judgment in one of the churches had been carved by St. Methodius himself on the occasion of the conversion of a Moravian prince. Peter was interested in purchasing it and had made preliminary arrangements with the Bürgermeister. In 1717, Field Marshal Prince Vasilii Dolgorukov asked Tatishchev to complete the arrangements when he was in Danzig. In the meantime, however, the city magistrates decided not to sell it to Peter because of criticism from the populace. In all likelihood, Tatishchev was greatly relieved, because he himself did not believe in the legend and thought the purchase unwise.

Tatishchev returned to Russia that fall with accomplishments on his first assignments that any veteran administrator would have been proud of. On 31 December, Bruce promoted him to the rank of lieutenant-captain and directed him to help plan the administration for the College of Mines and Manufactures.[23]

The College of Mines and Manufactures was one of the nine colleges or administrative bodies established by Peter the Great in December 1717 to replace the inefficient and overlapping system of *prikazi*.[24]

Similar to the Swedish administration at that time, Peter created separate colleges for Foreign Relations, State Revenue, Expenditure, Control, Justice, Army, Admiralty, Commerce, and Mines and Manufactures. Each college had a certain number of governing officials, and their respective presidents were equivalent to ministers in western

European nations and had seats in the Senate. Bruce, President of the College of Mines and Manufactures, was the only foreigner appointed to the highest post. Unfortunately, the exact nature and extent of Tatishchev's activity in the College is not known. It is known, however, that Bruce on one occasion trusted him to carry an administrative plan to Peter, who was then staying at Olonets.[25] No doubt, Tatishchev's knowledge of German and engineering qualified him for his work and made him a most useful assistant to Bruce, especially when one considers that Tatishchev was one of the few native Russians associated with the College. In all likelihood, he functioned in the capacity of secretary to Bruce.

In 1718, Tatishchev also aided Bruce when the Field Marshal was one of the chief negotiators at the Aland Congress, which had been called between Russia and Sweden to end the Great Northern War.[26] In fact, Tatishchev was in charge of finding a suitable place for the meetings; and, during the negotiations proper, he was entrusted with messages to carry between Bruce and Peter the Great. The talks dragged on until September 1719, when Sweden refused the Russian conditions and the Congress terminated.

Besides assisting Bruce with the administrative reforms, Tatishchev worked on his own project. On 18 March 1719, he presented to Peter a plan for a land survey of Russia.[27] First, he suggested that the Government inventory the property of all families to insure against fraudulent land transfers. He also proposed that all administrative areas be clearly marked off so that there would be no question of jurisdiction among local authorities, and that maps be drawn of the entire country showing natural land features as well as administrative boundaries. Tatishchev thereupon assured Peter that the cost of the project would be slight, and suggested that the land survey would decrease greed and enmity among people by removing the opportunities to acquire property fraudulently.

More important than the land survey project itself, Tatishchev's preparatory geographical work stimulated his interest in early Russian history. In noting the various land features and administrative districts, he became curious about their former names and the different peoples who occupied these places in ancient times.[28] He first turned to Polish and other foreign sources to find information about ancient Russia, but he soon found these inadequate. When he told Peter the Great about this problem, Peter told him about the existence of a copy of the Nestor chronicle in the Imperial Library. Tatishchev's examination of the manuscript marked the beginning of his lifelong interest in Russian history.

Shortly thereafter, however, he had to abandon work on the land survey project because his activities in the College of Mines and Manufactures occupied most of his time.[29] In the following spring, he was instructed to administer the State factory system in the Ural Mountains.

On 9 March 1720, the College of Mines and Manufactures commissioned V. N. Tatishchev, at the age of 34, lieutenant-captain, and instructed him to administer the State factory system in the Ural Mountains.[30] Specifically, Tatishchev was to increase production by constructing new factories closer to the iron mines, and to establish schools to train future craftsmen. The Saxon metallurgist Johann Bluher,[31] and mining engineers I. P. Patrushev and Gabriel Schornfelder accompanied him. On 31 July of that year, the party arrived in Kungur, center of the Urals metal industry.

Mining and metallurgy grew into important industries during the reign of Peter the Great, and the Ural region seemed to be the most promising site to establish metal works.[32] Two small smelting plants had been established in the 1630's, but these ceased to be operative at the end of the century. In the early 1690's, interest renewed in the Ural region when A. A. Vinius explored the possibilities of the area's manufacturing potential. However, it was Peter the Great himself who gave the real stimulus to Russia's metal production. When near Azov in June 1696, Peter inquired where deposits of iron ore could be found in Russia. He realized that the country needed its own independent source of high-grade ore for cannon and other military machines.

Several months later, in January 1697, Peter was informed that deposits of high-quality ore were located in the Chusavaia River region.[33] Within a month, Peter had the metal tested and found it suitable for the manufacture of cannon. Moreover, in April, Vinius wrote Peter, who was then abroad, about the advantages of starting an iron industry in the Urals. By the end of 1697, a metal processing plant was under construction at Alapaevsk.

When Peter returned from western Europe in August 1698, he devoted two weeks exclusively to planning factories in the Urals.[34] As a result of his work, the Neviansk factory was established in the following year and the Kamensk in March 1700. By the spring of 1701, the Neviansk plant was operational, and an Uktussk factory was established along the Iset River.

During the time that the State factories were being planned, N. A. Demidov, a factory owner in Tula, wanted to establish his own iron works in the Urals.[35] An expert metallurgist, Demidov quickly recognized the high potential of both the Ural region and the iron industry in Russia. On 10 February 1702, he asked Peter to turn the new Neviansk factory over to him. Peter was willing to do so because there was a shortage of metallurgists in Russia, and he knew that Demidov was a competent factory manager. Permission was granted that March.

Demidov quickly built his own metallurgical empire in the Urals. In April 1703, he asked for and received permission to expand his enterprise by building other factories in the Kungur region.[36] Moreover, he secured several privileges from the State, such as unlimited use of lumber and ores and the right to possess runaway serfs and employ them in his factories.[37] For all practical purposes, Demidov soon had a monopoly on the production of iron, though he had to turn over to the State factories ten percent of the mined ore. But, while Demidov's enterprise was running at full capacity, the State factories operated inefficiently— when they were operating at all. However, in December 1719, the College of Mines and Manufactures, fearing that Russia's iron production might fall into the hands of one man, decided to increase the output of the State factory system.[38] It was Peter the Great who selected V. N. Tatishchev for this most important task.

Tatishchev's plans for increasing production consisted of establishing one large factory complex which would serve as a center for the Ural industry.[39] The new plant was to operate continuously and to be centrally located among factories already established. On 2 January 1721, Tatishchev instructed Timofei Burtsov, manager of the Uktussk factory, to ask his craftmen where they thought the new plant should be located. Tatishchev explained that the new location should be suitable for construction of four furnaces, and not be more than ten *versts*[40] from the Uktussk plant. Also, lumber and iron mines must be readily accessible.

Within a short time, Burtsov gave Tatishchev the choices of the Uktussk workers, who favored two places situated along the Iset River.[41] One, the more preferable, was six versts from Uktussk, and the second was only three or four versts away. Burtsov suggested that Tatishchev should consider the number of mills, as well as furnaces, he wanted to construct in deciding between the sites. Tatishchev opted for the first preference of the Uktussk craftsmen for his future city, called Ekaterinburg[42] in honor of Peter the Great's wife and the future Empress of Russia. The location was ideal for lumber resources, and near iron mines.

The Soviet scholar M. A. Gorlovskii criticized Tatishchev for asking the Uktussk workers to find the location of the factory rather than seeking one himself as his previous biographers have claimed.[43] Certainly, Tatishchev's use of the workers' advice speaks well for his administrative ability. In short, by January 1721, Tatishchev had been in the Urals for only five months, and it is impossible that he could have known

11

more about the region than did the workers who had lived there for many years. Moreover, the craftsmen were closely acquainted with the specific problems and advantages of metallurgy in the Urals. Therefore, rather than embarking on a costly and time-consuming survey of the area himself, Tatishchev recognized that his best course of action was to obtain the advice and assistance of those who already knew the region.

On 6 February, Tatishchev sent his plans for the new factory to Bruce in St. Petersburg.[44] First, he called attention to the great importance that the new factory would have for Russia. He told the College of Mines and Manufactures that the new complex of 4 furnaces and 40 mills would insure a half-capacity production throughout the year. He then requested that craftsmen be sent from the Petersburg factories to the Urals and, at the same time, sought permission to hire free laborers rather than use serfs, noting that wage earners worked more efficiently. Since Ekaterinburg was to become the new industrial center, Tatishchev recommended that the Irbit Fair be transferred to his new city in order to stimulate commerce and provide wares for the workers. He estimated the cost of the construction at 25,000 rubles.

To avoid delay, Tatishchev immediately began to make preparations for construction. In fact, when he wrote Burtsov inquiring about a location, he instructed the Uktussk workers to start collecting bricks, lumber, and carts for the new factory.[45] Later in February, he ordered one Bukharov of the Uktussk plant to go to Tobol'sk and Verkhotursk factories to hire wage workers for construction. By early March, the men had cleared the area and had set up huts for supplies and living quarters. Tatishchev wrote the College of Mines and Manufactures again on the 21st inquiring about the delay of confirmation of his construction plans.

On 23 May, the College informed Tatishchev that they had rejected his plan because of its great cost, and ordered that construction be stopped.[46] Disappointed, to be sure, Tatishchev then prepared an alternative project. Instead of building a large complex, he suggested that they permit him to construct a small factory; that is, one consisting of only two furnaces and four mills. This project would cost only 4,000 rubles.

The exact reason for the College's rejection of Tatishchev's project is not known. Gorlovskii, for one, believed that the College of Mines and Manufactures, composed chiefly of foreigners, was not really interested in increasing Russia's iron production.[47] But these were the same officials who had decided to raise the State system's output in December 1719. Moreover, had not Tatishchev been a favorite of Bruce, trusted friend of Peter the Great, and, above all, a proven administrator? In all probability, the real reason for the rejection can be found in the intrigues of N. A. Demidov to have Tatishchev removed from the Urals region. Demidov worked through his close friend, Count Fëder Matveevich Apraksin, who was President of the College of the Admiralty.[48] Through Apraksin, Demidov complained to the College of Mines and Manufactures and to Peter the Great that Tatishchev had committed misdemeanors in his administration and had accepted bribes.

As the Government representative in the Urals, Tatishchev had authority to inspect all factories; that is, both the State works and those privately owned—Demidov's. When inspecting one of Demidov's plants, he noticed that the workers were using asbestos in the process without having first secured permission from the State.[49] He also would listen to the complaints of Demidov's serf laborers. The issues, to be sure, were minor. In fact, it is hardly conceivable that the Government would deny Demidov permission for using asbestos, and Demidov could easily have ignored Tatishchev's recommendations concerning his own serfs' complaints. But Demidov, above all, resented the fact that V. N. Tatishchev —his junior and inferior—could inspect his factories.

When Tatishchev went to Petersburg in January 1722 to inquire about the rejection of his projects, the College of Mines and Manufactures decided to send Georg Hennin to Kungur, center of the Urals metal industry, with full authority to investigate Demidov's charges and to take over the administration.[50] Born in Nassau, Hennin came to Russia in 1698 to begin a career in the service as an artillery instructor. Later, he helped establish several factories in St. Petersburg; and, in 1716, he founded a school at Olonets to teach mathematics, engineering, and artillery to children of poor landowners.

After arriving in the Urals, Hennin personally went to Demidov to inquire into the exact nature of his charges against Tatishchev.[51] All that Demidov would say was that Tatishchev had insulted him, and he absolutely refused to write his complaints on paper since he did not consider Tatishchev his equal. Sometime later, Hennin sent an emissary to Demidov, who finally charged Tatishchev with having sequestered part of a wharf on the Chusovoi River and charged toll fees on supplies transported to Demidov's factory.

A hearing was held that fall, and the charges against Tatishchev were dropped. Tatishchev, to be sure, did sequester the wharf and charge toll fees on Demidov's supplies—but he did so on orders from M. A. Cherkasskii, the Governor of Siberia.[52] The bribery charges were also dropped; Demidov himself had tried to bribe Tatishchev—unsuccessfully.

On 17 December, Hennin wrote Peter the Great telling him of his

13

personal happiness that Tatishchev was acquitted.[53] He approved of Tatishchev's plans for Ekaterinburg and requested 30,000 rubles to continue construction. As for Tatishchev's administrative ability, Hennin wrote: "He knows everything concerning the construction of factories; and he does it so easily, and I see that he is willing and skillful in it."[54]

Although Hennin remained in the Urals as chief administrator, it was Tatishchev, along with five others, who directed the construction of Ekaterinburg.[55] In fact, it was Tatishchev, with the help of two students from the Moscow Artillery School, who designed the factory machinery. Also, during his stay in the Urals, Tatishchev established two schools to provide a basic education for those who intended to enter the military, and two others to train metallurgists and mining engineers.[56] Moreover, he increased the efficiency of the postal system to improve connections with European Russia, and encouraged the growth of home industry. He returned to St. Petersburg at the end of 1723 to present new plans to the College of Mines and Manufactures.

While Tatishchev was in the capital in 1724, Peter the Great took the opportunity to ask him about the validity of Demidov's accusations.[57] Tatishchev remained calm and answered Peter by quoting Saint Paul: "The reward given to one who works to earn it is not reckoned as a favour, it is reckoned as his due." (Romans IV, 4) Peter said that he did not understand. Tatishchev continued by explaining that he did accept "remunerations" when he was judging cases, but that "remunerations" were not the same as "usury" or "bribe taking." For example, when Tatishchev saw that a complaint was obviously invalid, he would postpone the case until the plaintiff withdrew the charge at his own cost. This procedure allowed time to consider the more important cases and ensured justice, especially since legal procedure often protected the guilty. At the same time, Tatishchev reasoned there was no reason why he would not accept "remunerations" for settling a case in the same way in which he would have done otherwise, ". . . persuaded as I am that neither divine justice, nor that of your Majesty can condemn this manner of acting."[58] Peter then understood what Tatishchev meant by quoting Saint Paul, and he approved of his accepting "remunerations." He cautioned, however, that, in the hands of the unloyal, this practice could be harmful to the State.

If Tatishchev's explanation was humorous, it was also cunning. Similar to Dolgorukii's situation in 1717, Tatishchev knew exactly what the Emperor wanted to hear. Tatishchev did not receive "remunerations" for his own benefit. He accepted them because they expedited justice and permitted him to carry out his tasks more efficiently.

14

Although Tatishchev devoted almost all of his time to administrative duties during these years, he also managed to pursure his interests in early Russian history. In 1720, he found another (Raskol'nichie) manuscript of the Nestor chronicle, which varied significantly from the one which he received earlier from Peter the Great.[59] These differences encouraged him to search for other documents on Russian history in Siberia. Also, in 1722, Peter gave him the Murom chronicle, which Tatishchev described as useful but full of fables.[60]

Tatishchev's first assignment of major importance can be regarded as an administrative success. Although he had been in the Urals for only a short time, he brought both direction and efficiency to the State factory system. Moreover, Tatishchev's plans for an industrial complex on the Iset were strongly approved by his successor Hennin. To be sure, it was Tatishchev who directed the early stages of construction of Ekaterinburg and who designed the factory machinery. Perhaps, too, a good measure of his success can be seen in the Demidov affair. Although the dispute ostensibly grew out of a personal issue, it is highly probable that Demidov considered Tatishchev's efficient management of the State factory system a threat to his own industrial empire.

Tatishchev spent most of the next year, 1723, at court, where he probably attended the coronation of Peter's wife as Empress and occupied himself researching in early Russian history.[61]

There can be no doubt that as an administrator Tatishchev had already proven himself as a most useful servant to the State. He owed his rapid rise in State service to his ability to accomplish assignments to the complete satisfaction of his superiors. He was at the center of activity of Peter the Great's reform work, and he associated with those who most ardently supported it. In fact, he was in the presence of the Emperor from time to time.

More important, he soon developed a *Weltanschauung* particularly suited to the new Petrine civil service. Looking back upon these years in his *Testament*, Tatishchev related to his son Evgraf:

> Obedience consists in two things, to refuse nothing and to ask nothing; this is secret of a contented life. This also is the doctrine of Saint Paul and of his divine Master; it ought to be our rule of conduct. But as our weakness prefers example to precept, I will place before you one in my own experience. It was in 1704, the year of my departure for service. My father, in bidding me farewell, recommended me strongly never to decline any charge however unpleasant it might be, and never to seek one. Well, every time that I followed this counsel, I felt happy even in the midst of the greatest vexations, and never have I refused anything or

asked anything without having afterwards repented. And others have experienced the same thing.[62]

Although Tatishchev's admonition represented traditional values, it had a new importance for him. With the creation of the civil service, Tatishchev found himself in a new society. He acquired his own social position through performance in State service, and his maxim well suited his new milieu. Tatishchev soon identified himself within the new system, and personally supported the Petrine reforms.

Chapter III

Assignment in Sweden

The need for trained metallurgists and mining engineers increased as Russia's metal industry grew during the Petrine era. Since Russia could not fill the demand and did not possess the necessary facilities, Georg Hennin suggested that Russian students train in Sweden. Peter the Great sent V. N. Tatishchev to Sweden to make the necessary arrangements. While he was establishing contacts there, Tatishchev availed himself of information gathered by Swedish scholars on early Russian history.

In September 1724, Hennin addressed an inquiry to the College of Mines and Manufactures about the possibility of young Russians' being sent to Sweden to study metallurgy.[1] On the 23rd, the College sent Hennin's inquiry to the Senate, which in turn forwarded it to the College of Foreign Affairs. The Senate then instructed Ambassador Bestuzhev in Stockholm to ascertain whether the Swedish Government would be willing to accept Russian students. There was good reason for such formalities. The Great Northern War had ended only three years earlier, and enmity, not to mention suspicion, still existed between Sweden and Russia.

Peter the Great, however, did not wait for Bestuzhev's reply.[2] He realized the importance of having Russians learn metallurgy and engineering in the schools of the world's leading iron producer. He first spoke with the Swedish Ambassador in St. Petersburg and, after a favorable response, promoted his trusted friend V. N. Tatishchev to the civilian rank of Collegial Counselor[3] in preparation for sending him to Sweden. On 1 October, he sent a decree to the Senate which provided that 22 students from the Moscow Artillery School who were knowledgeable in mathematics and related subjects be sent to Sweden.[4] At the same time, he instructed Ambassador Bestuzhev to inquire of the Swedish Government whether they would permit their craftsmen to work in Russia.

Peter had definite reasons for sending Tatishchev to Sweden as well as the 22 students; namely, Peter wanted to have an expert examine the Swedish mines and metal works and note their metallurgical processes.[5] Tatishchev was also to be in charge of enrolling the Russian students in the various training schools and factories. At the same time, Peter instructed Tatishchev to study the Swedish monetary and commercial systems. Last, but not least, he ordered Tatishchev "to observe and to inform [him] on the political situation, overt acts and secret intentions of that [Swedish] government."[6] On 29 October, Peter informed Bestuzhev of his decision to send Tatishchev to Stockholm, and ordered him to help his emissary in every way possible. Tatishchev left St. Petersburg at the end of that month.

Tatishchev arrived in Stockholm on 7 December, and immediately began his assignment by discussing the Swedish monetary system at some length with one Count Bonde.[7] On 2 January, he wrote I. A. Cherkasov, who was in charge of his correspondence to the Emperor, recommending that the decimal system be introduced into Russia for currency and for weights and measures. Also, during his first month abroad, Tatishchev studied mechanical designs and spent two weeks contacting metallurgical experts and mining engineers who would be willing to train the Russians. Most of them were willing to receive the students, but they claimed that permission from the Swedish Government was necessary. Bestuzhev cleared up this formality with the Swedish Senate. Tatishchev, however, found the second part of his task impossible; the Swedish Government prohibited its craftsmen from serving in foreign countries. Bestuzhev somehow had neglected to inform St. Petersburg of this matter.

During the winter of 1725, Tatishchev visited several of Sweden's more important mines and metallurgical plants, including those at Salberg, Avstafor, Stalheim, and Bervfors.[8] He also inspected the Chevel and Falun iron-copper works and requested money from the College of Mines and Manufactures to purchase diagrams of the factory machinery. He later informed Hennin that he held several conversations with the expert metallurgists Nolheim, Dur, and Nielson, and had obtained drawings of the machinery at Falun through its foreman, Heisler.[9] He then asked Hennin to support a request for 300 rubles to travel to Saxony, where it would be possible to hire craftsmen for the Russian service. The large sum was needed, he explained, to buy gifts for the metallurgists, since most looked upon Russia as the least desirable country in which to work. The College, however, refused to supply the necessary funds; in fact, Tatishchev experienced many difficulties with the College after the death of Peter the Great in January.

Although official assignments occupied most of his time, Tatishchev also managed to pursue his interests in history. In his first report to St. Petersburg, he mentioned that he had heard that there were many sources on early Russian history nearby. "And if your Majesty permits,

18

I hope to visit these people, who collected these [and placed them] in order, for I have friends among professors and historians here."[10] He said that his friend Tabbert von Strahlenberg had written a history of Siberia with maps. During his stay with Strahlenberg, Tatishchev made notes and corrections on the manuscript and tried to persuade the author to dedicate the work to Peter the Great.[11] Strahlenberg, however, eventually published his *Der Nord und ostliche Theil von Europa* in 1730 with a dedication to the Swedish King.

Tatishchev also had the opportunity to make the acquaintance of other Swedish scholars. While still in Stockholm, he met Heinrich Brenner, who was an authority on Oriental languages. More important to Tatishchev, Brenner was an official of the Royal Library and a member of the Swedish Society of Antiquities. He informed Tatishchev of many documents on ancient history and gained for him access to the Library.[12]

Through Brenner, he met Professor Ericus Erici Benzelius, who was considered an authority on the early history of the North.[13] Benzelius informed Tatishchev about the many sources on Russian history available in the Upsala Library and he promised his recent acquaintance that he would obtain permission for him to use them. Tatishchev, to be sure, discussed Russian history with Benzelius and won the Swedish scholar's respect. Sometime during that spring, he wrote a study under Benzelius' direction entitled "Generossis Dn. Basilii Tatishchow Epistola ad D. Ericum Benzilium de mamontowa kost, id est, de ossibus bestiae Mamont dictae."[14] The work concerned mammoth remains which Tatishchev found during his stay in Siberia; it was published later in Sweden and England.

By mid-spring 1725, Tatishchev had already absorbed some important aspects of Swedish research into Russian history. In a letter of 9 April to I. A. Cherkasov, he explained that most Swedish historians believed that the capital of the early Russian princes was located in the Ladoga region.[15] They also mentioned that there were many connections between Scandinavia and Russia during this time. Later, in May, he informed Cherkasov that he had found a particularly good source on ancient Russian history which was written in Latin.[16] He explained that the book had been written by a Swede who lived in Russia for some time, but that the work was never published due to the recent war. He said that he was trying to find someone to translate it into Russian. In his next letter to Cherkasov, he included a synopsis or table of contents of a history which he was having translated; it is not clear, however, whether this was the same work to which he referred earlier.[17] Nevertheless, the work, entitled *Conspectus spicilegii antiquitatum Russicarum ex His-*

toriis praecipue Gothicis et Iflandicis, covered the history of several of
such early Russian peoples as the Scythians, Sarmatians, and Venedi.
More important, it included a section on "Garodoriki," which Tatishchev
explained was a city or realm near Lake Ladoga which had been destroyed; Novgorod the Great was built in its place. He closed the letter
by saying that he wished to have a hundred rubles to buy more books
on Russian history.

Through Benzelius, Tatishchev also met Eric Björner, who was Secretary of the Society of Antiquities at Upsala.[18] Björner was a noted
geographer, and just the year before, 1724, he had led an expedition to
northern Sweden, where he found several Runic stones and other ancient
monuments. He was also researching ancient Scandinavian history.
Tatishchev discussed with him various connections between the ancient
Scandinavians and Russians he had heard about from Benzelius. In fact,
several years later, Björner published a book on the very subject, entitled
*Schediasma historico-geographicum de Varegis, heroibus Scandianis et
primus Russiae dynastis, quo licuit studio exhibitum ab E. J. Bioerner.*
In this work, Björner traced the genealogies of the Scandinavian princes
from the Varangian Tryggve, who lived in the sixth century, to
Herander or Riurik, who lived in the eighth,[19] and concluded that the
Rus were a Scandinavian people who inhabited "Malaia Riuzalandiia" in
the Ladoga region. Tatishchev took notes on Björner's research.[20]

In an undated letter of 1725 to Cherkasov, Tatishchev included "A
Short Summary of Russian History," in which he tried to summarize
his findings in Sweden.[21] He began by noting that one Magog, son of
Iafetov, was the great-great-grandfather of the European peoples. After
confusing several peoples, such as the Scythians with the Goths, he
mentioned that the "Rossiane" appeared in the fifth century and later,
under the names of "Roksolany" and "Moskvitiane," lived in the land
of the Slavs. They were called "Ruskii" and their land "Rossiia" in
the eighth century, after the river Rus. Although his description of the
ancient Russian peoples appears confusing, it demonstrates that he had
absorbed a certain amount of the Scandinavian scholarship on the subject. Furthermore, since we do not know the exact date of the letter,
he may well have written it during the early stage of his research. The
main point, however, is that he rceognized that there was a great gap in
Russia's knowledge of its own past.

The Russian students from the Moscow Artillery School arrived that
November, and Tatishchev was ordered to assign them to their respective schools and teachers.[22] The College of Mines and Manufactures gave
him 2,148 rubles for their expenses, and instructed him to return to

20

Russia directly afterwards. Before he returned, however, he submitted another request for funds; the College again outrightly refused him. In fact, this time they accused Tatishchev of having squandered on "whims" the money that had been given to him. Even though Ambassador Golovin, Bestuzhev's recent replacement in Stockholm, defended Tatishchev's expenditures, the members of the College of Mines and Manufactures did not yield. They sent him only enough money for the return trip.

When he returned to Russia in the spring of 1726, he submitted a list of expenses amounting to 588 rubles.[23] Quite interestingly, although Tatishchev purchased books on mechanics and various diagrams, most of the entires were for the purchase of materials on Russian history, including chronicles, books, and several translations. In all likelihood, the College had the latter purchases in mind when referring to Tatishchev's squandering funds. In June, he gave a formal account of his assignment to the members of the College, and, in October, wrote a report for Empress Catherine.[24]

The College's refusal to send Tatishchev more funds and, even more so, the accusations of squandering—that is, spending—money on historical sources, were indications of a change of attitude in the Russian capital. Tatishchev recognized this state of affairs as early as the spring of 1725, when he wrote to Empress Catherine in explanation of his mission in Sweden. He told the Empress that her late husband had instructed him to place 22 students in metallurgical schools and to hire Swedish craftsmen for service in Russia. At the same time, he mentioned that he had met Professor Benzelius and that he read books and other materials on Russian history in the Upsala Library. He closed the letter by pointing out that he had been prevented from hiring craftsmen in Sweden, and, therefore, he requested 300 rubles to travel to Saxony for this purpose. Obviously, either the Empress chose to ignore the request or the College of Mines and Manufactures overruled her.

Indeed, much had changed in St. Petersburg after Tatishchev's departure in October 1724. Because of his enthusiasm for the growth of metallurgy in Russia, Peter the Great was willing to grant his loyal servant anything necessary to accomplish his assignment. There would have been no question of his receiving the 300 rubles to go to Saxony. Moreover, from Tatishchev's letter of 18 December, Peter must have been well aware of his researching ancient Russian history in his spare time. To be sure, there is every indication that the Emperor would have wholeheartedly approved of this activity. After all, had he not encouraged Tatishchev's research earlier by providing him with sources in 1719 and 1722? Perhaps the reason for Tatishchev's difficulty in obtaining funds was that the members of the College of Mines and Manufactures were mostly engineers and metallurgists and lacked interest in history.

Tatishchev's research in early Russian history during his stay in Sweden has a greater importance in Russian historiography than even he was aware of. In spite of the apparent confusion in his letters, the main element of his research was that in early times Scandinavians maintained contact with the cities, "Gorodoriki," in the Ladoga region. Moreover, he learned that the Varangian Rus were a Scandinavian people and that they inhabited the area called "Malaia Riuzalandiia" in the time of Riurik. This account by Swedish scholars apparently verified and expanded for him the story he found in the Nestor chronicle about the Slavic peoples' calling Riurik to rule them.

By the second half of the eighteenth century, this account of the "calling of Riurik" became known as the "Norman Theory."[25] In its various forms, the Norman Theory states that the Varangian Rus were a Scandinavian people, and infers that there was a distinct Teutonic influence in the formation of the Russian monarchy and State. Besides the reference to the Varangian Rus in the Nestor chronicle, Normanists at first emphasized the presence of words of Scandinavian origin in the language of Kiev. However, by the end of the nineteenth century, this list of words was greatly reduced. Other more recent information has also discredited the Norman Theory. There is very little evidence of Scandinavian influence on early Russian folklore, and none on the Kievan law codes. Moreover, Arabic accounts which referred to the Rus considered them a Slavic people in southern Russia, and not a Scandinavian group or Viking detachment.

Although some of the chief arguments for the Norman Theory have suffered in recent times, some historians continue to accept it as being essentially valid. Many who have supported the theory over the past two centuries have emphasized the role Scandinavians apparently played in regard to the formation of the first state in Russia. Others have argued against the thesis by claiming that the first government in Russia had a Slavic origin, and that the whole account of the Scandinavian Varangian Rus is, invalid. The debate continues today.

According to Russian historiographical tradition, the German scholar Göttlieb Siegfried Bayer has been credited, or discredited, with discovering the main elements of the Norman Theory and introducing it into Russia. After completing studies in classics at Königsburg in 1726, Bayer acquired a position as classicist and orientalist in the newly formed

Academy of Sciences in St. Petersburg. He formulated his thesis in the 1740's. Later, the German historian Gerhard Friedrich Müller supported Bayer's thesis in debates with M. V. Lomonosov, who argued that the Varangian Rus were a Slavic people.[26] At that point, the Norman Theory became an integral and hotly contested part of Russian historiography.

Both Bayer and Müller knew Tatishchev in the 1720's and early 1730's, and knew of his research in early Russian history. In fact, Tatishchev interested Bayer in early Russian chronicles and helped him work with them.[27] From all indications, it seems that Tatishchev rather than Bayer should be credited or discredited with bringing the substance of the subsequent Norman Theory to Russia.[28] He studied early chronicles and absorbed Swedish scholarship on the Varangian Rus before Bayer and Müller formulated their ideas on the subject. Tatishchev, however, never considered his research on the Varangians as the Norman Theory, with all of its ethnic and nationalist overtones. Indeed, this debate began after his death in 1750. Tatishchev merely thought he was bringing useful information to Russia to fill a gap in its early history. To be sure, it is possible that Bayer could have interested himself in and researched the topic on his own. That conjecture, however, cannot obscure the fact that V. N. Tatishchev discovered and made available to him information on early Russian history which later became an important issue in Russian historiography.

Chapter IV

The "Learned Guard"

Peter the Great's death in 1725 marked the end of an era. The absence of a single and powerful will to impose modernization on Russia permitted some members of the traditional nobility to slow down the pace of reform.[1] They wanted a respite to adjust to the new ways and society created in the process of westernization. The absence of a strong monarch also permitted nests of intriguers such as Prince A. D. Menshikov and the princely families of Dolgorukii and Golitsyn to surround the throne in places once occupied by loyal friends and State servants.

V. N. Tatishchev's first years and experiences in State service had molded him into a new type of person. Even though he was the son of a nobleman, Tatishchev soon identified himself and his accomplishments with the Petrine system. Now that less ardent supporters of modernization had reasserted their influence, he no longer fitted into the society of traditional courtiers and opportunists who were near the throne after Peter's death. Supporters of the Petrine reform work, such as V. N. Tatishchev, were unwelcome in the new royal entourage of intriguers and cabal plotters.

The siutation, however, was complicated with the problem of orderly succession to the throne.[2] In his decree of 5 February 1722, Peter the Great abolished primogeniture and established the right to choose his own successor.[3] However, Peter died on 27 January 1725 without designating an heir to the throne. By the next day, Prince D. M. Golitsyn and Count P. A. Tolstoi convinced the Senate, the Synod, and the Generality (holders of the first four ranks in the Petrine table of ranks) that Catherine should succeed her husband. They reasoned that Peter had indicated her his choice when he had her crowned "Empress" in 1724.

Empress Catherine, however, cared little for governing Russia, and preferred to spend most of her time drinking and pursuing other pleasures. Right from the beginning of her reign, she left all government matters to the President of the Army College, Prince A. D. Menshikov. Although Menshikov had been a loyal supporter of Peter the

Great, he now saw that he could be sovereign of Russia in everything but name. In order to legalize his authority, he created the Supreme Privy Council by decree in February 1726. With Menshikov as head, the Council consisted of Prince A. M. Apraksin, who was President of the Admiralty College; Counts G. U. Golovkin and P. A. Tolstoi; Baron A. I. Osterman; and Prince D. M. Golitsyn. The Supreme Privy Council thenceforth functioned as the legislative authority in the name of the Empress. With the exception of Prince Golitsyn, who represented the old Muscovite nobility, all were associates of Peter the Great and wished to continue his reform work.

Although the Council appeared to have been a "progressive" body, it was merely the tool of the ambitious Menshikov. In fact, the Council convened only once in the next year, on the occasion of the Empress' death.[4] Menshikov gained complete control of the Government by depriving the Senate of administrative functions when its Chief Procurator, P. I. Iaguzhinskii, opposed his policies. Iaguzhinskii was removed from the Senate and relegated to the post of royal equerry.

Menshikov's position, however, still was not secure. Catherine's health was weakened by her constant drinking, and Menshikov had to seek other means to retain control in the event of her death. After an abortive attempt to gain the throne of Courland for himself, he schemed to have Catherine's proposed successor, the future Emperor Peter II, marry his daughter Maria. He obtained Catherine's permission for the nuptials in March 1727.

Menshikov's plans matured none too soon. Catherine died only two months later. The Supreme Privy Council met for the first time to promulgate her "testament." She willed that Peter, grandson of Peter the Great and son of Tsarevich Alexis, was to succeed her. Because of his minority (he was only 11 years old at that time), she established a regency consisting of the Supreme Privy Council and Duke Charles Frederick of Holstein, husband of her sister Anne. Moreover, she stipulated that Peter was to marry Maria Menshikov. The Duke of Holstein thereupon became a member of the Privy Council.

Even though Catherine designated the Supreme Privy Council—and the Duke of Holstein—as regents, Menshikov was still ruler of Russia. Menshikov took the boy Emperor into his house, where he kept him virtually prisoner. Nevertheless, the succession of an 11-year-old provided the opportunity for others to challenge Menshikov's position.

Every ancient family, on this account flattered itself with the hopes of getting into this young Prince's favor. The Lapouchins [Lopukhins], the

Soltikoffs [Saltikovs], being near relations to the Emperor, imagined this gave them a right to aspire to the first places, but they were all deceived. The Princes Dolgorouki [Dolgorukii], some of whom were more immediately about the Emperor's person, had availed themselves of the moment, and had, as one may say, seized all the avenues to the Emperor's ear.[5]

By the end of summer 1727, Menshikov began to lose influence. General Manstein, who was in Russian service at that time, related that the all-powerful Privy Councilor brought about his own downfall.[6] It seemed that when Peter II gave his sister a gift of 9,000 ducats, Menshikov seized the purse. Peter heard of this and took offense at the transgression on his royal will. In the meantime, the Princes Dolgorukii and Baron Osterman, who was Peter's tutor, told the child that Menshikov was instrumental in the death of his father.[7] Whatever the real circumstances, in September 1727, Menshikov was deprived of his place in the Privy Council and exiled to Siberia.

Almost as quickly as Menshikov was "dethroned," the Dolgorukii family, scions of the old Muscovite nobility, won influence over the Emperor. Like Menshikov, they kept Peter in their home and let none but their ilk have access to him. "Everything was left to them. The Emperor frequented none but the Dolgorouckis [Dolgorukiis]; and no one even durst approach him without their consent."[8] In February 1728, Princes Alexis and V. L. Dolgorukii became members of the Supreme Privy Council; and another, Prince Ivan, was favored with the title of ober-chamberlain. To repeat another of Menshikov's schemes, they tried to secure their position through marriage. On 19 November, they betrothed the 13-year-old Emperor to Prince Alexis' 17-year-old daughter Catherine.

There was nothing but feasts and rejoicing for the rest of the year 1729, and 1730. The Dolgoroucki [Dolgorukii] family now imagined they had surmounted all obstacles, and proposed to have the nuptials consummated in a few days; reckoning thereby to have nothing to fear in the future from their enemies and their cabals.[9]

The energy once directed to administrative reform and to westernization was now dissipated in court intrigues and in disdain for the new customs introduced by Peter the Great. Almost as if to symbolize the latter, the court returned to the old capital, Moscow, in January of 1728.

But, in spite of the political situation—or perhaps because of it—Manstein has recorded that many Russians living in that era considered this period the happiest of times.

Even at this instant all Russia pronounces this epoch the happiest that it had ever known for a century past. There was no compulsion to serve in the army, so that everyone could stay at home quietly, enjoy his property, and even improve it. Except a few of the great, who were jealous of the power of the Dolgorouckis [Dolgorukiis], all the rest of the nation were content.[10]

If these five years were the happiest of times for some Russians, they were the saddest for those who wished to continue the Petrine reform work. Now that individuals such as V. N. Tatishchev and his friend Archbishop of Novgorod Theofan Prokopovich were unwelcome at court, they turned their energies chiefly to intellectual pursuits. They spent most of their time discussing the ideas and major works of the early Enlightenment with the members of the recently established Academy of Sciences.[11] In short, their ambitions were to "enlighten" Russia with education and the philosophies of the Enlightenment and to revive the reform work of Peter the Great's reign. The activities of the "Learned Guard,"[12] as the Archbishop, Tatishchev, and Prince A. D. Kantemir referred to themselves, soon evoked a swarm of criticism from the Privy Council and other members of the old Muscovite nobility.

Archbishop Theofan, the oldest member of the Learned Guard, was born to a family of merchants in Kiev in 1681.[13] He received his early education at the Mogila Academy in Kiev and in Poland, where he converted temporarily to the Uniat rite. Afterwards, he studied the classics, philosophy, history, and theology at the Jesuit College of St. Athanasius in Rome. In 1704, he returned to Kiev, where he taught rhetoric, theology, and philosophy at the Mogila Academy. Although Theofan took Holy Orders sometime before he returned to Russia, he never neglected his interest in secular education. In 1705, he wrote a work on esthetics, *De Arte Poetica*, and later, a tragicomedy in classical form, *Vladimir*.[14] The plot of Prince Vladimir's bringing Christianity to Russia in the tenth century was really a subtle praise of Peter the Great's bringing westernization in his generation.[15] By this time, too, Theofan was well read in the major thinkers of the seventeenth century, including Pufendorf, Hobbes, Bacon, and Grotius.

In 1709, on the occasion of the Russian victory over the Swedes at Poltava, Theofan, then prefect of the theological academy, delivered a sermon praising the feat when Peter and his army were near Kiev. In 1711, Peter called the young cleric to join him on the Pruth Campaign, after which Theofan became one of his most trusted advisors. In 1715, Peter invited Theofan to his new capital, where the young clergyman

27

was placed in charge of publishing works of western European thinkers in translation.

In 1718, when Peter the Great was having difficulties with his son Alexis, Theofan delivered a "Sermon on Royal Authority and Honor," in which he argued that Government authority was established by God and, therefore, should be obeyed by everyone.[16] In his sermon, Theofan cited numerous examples from Scripture and challenged the right of individuals to plot to overthrow authority: "Nay more—they know not that the highest power is established and armed with the sword of God and that to oppose it is a sin against God Himself. . . ."[17] At the same time, he said that even the clergy must obey secular authority and not follow the example of the Roman Church and its papacy, which set itself beyond the jurisdiction of lay government.

Theofan also justified the supremacy of secular authority through natural law.

> And behold, might there not be in the number of natural laws this one, too, that there are to be authorities holding power among nations? There is indeed! And this is the very chief of all laws. . . . From this, then, it is likewise evident that Nature teaches us too of the obedience due to authorities. Look within yourself and consider this: Governmental authority is necessary to natural law.[18]

He also dismissed the argument that people do not have to obey an unjust government by reminding his listeners that all governments, bad as well as good ones, were God's "anointed": "And that is the fact that the Scriptures order obedience not only to the good powers, but also to the perverse and the faithless ones."[19]

Concerning the specific situation at hand, Theofan was boundless in his admiration for Peter the Great. In Peter's reform work, he saw the "enlightening" of Russia through education. He then accused those who wished to destroy Peter's achievements of wanting to plunge Russia into darkness. To Theofan, Peter was the prophet without honor in his own country.

> All state obligations depend on two things, on the civil, I say, and the military. Who in our land has ever managed these two as well as this man? Renewed Russia in everything, or rather given her a new birth? What then is to be his reward from us? For it was by his providence and his own labors that everyone received glory and freedom from care, while he himself has a shameful name and a life of misery? What a scandal this is. . . . Glorious among foreigners, dishonored among his own![20]

28

He then observed that, although Russians always had a tradition of obedience to their monarch, there were now groups who wanted to dethrone Peter and destroy his reform work. He, therefore, warned that, if they succeeded, Russia would again experience a time of troubles, when the country would turn into a land of pillage and murder. "Where and when has the scepter been transferred by force without a great deal of blood, sacrifice of the best men, the destruction of great houses?"[21]

Five years later, in 1722, when Peter the Great altered succession from primogeniture to proclamation, Theofan defended his decision in a tract entitled *Right of the Monarch's Will*.[22] Although his argument ran similar to his earlier "Sermon," Theofan relied more on natural law theory and history. His sources were primarily Pufendorf, Hobbes, and Grotius. After some general remarks about government authority, he enumerated Aristotle's three forms of government—aristocracy, democracy, and monarchy—and proceeded to describe the strengths and weaknesses of each. He explained the advantages and disadvantages of inherited and elected monarchies, and concluded that an inherited monarchy had always been in accord with the will of the Russian people. He then presented numerous examples from history of the various ways monarchical authority has been passed on, beginning with the rulers of ancient Persia and continuing through the Roman emperors to the kings of medieval England. From natural law theory and from the examples of history, Theofan concluded that, since monarchical authority is the highest authority, the sovereign could bequeath his rule to whomever he chose. In fact, if the monarch saw that his proposed successor was not fit to rule, he should seek another who was better suited to the task.

Besides being a loyal supporter of Peter the Great's policies, Theofan also was an important clergyman in the Orthodox Church. In 1718, he was appointed Bishop of Pskov, and, seven years later, Archbishop of Novgorod, a post which he held until his death. He also participated in the revision of the clergy, and, in 1721, wrote the "Ecclesiastical Regulation" which abolished the Patriarchate and established the Holy Synod.

The Ecclesiastical Regulation set up a new Church administration similar to the recently introduced collegiate system for State administration.[23] Rather than a Patriarchate, the Church was to be ruled by a body composed of a lay Procurator and clergymen in the posts of President, Vice President, and various councilors. In the Regulation, Theofan issued instructions for the education of churchmen. He recommended that clerical students study grammar, geography, and history, as well as philosophy and theology. Last, but not least, he considered the study of

Pufendorf's political ideas most important. In short, the Ecclesiastical Regulation brought the Orthodox Church to conform with the wishes of the Russian Government. In this sense, there is much truth in the argument that it "Protestantized" Orthodoxy. Theofan served in the Synod as Vice President.

In July 1726, the Synod was divided into two departments, one for administration and the other in charge of finance.[24] Theofan worked with Anastasii Kondoides in the administrative division, concerning himself with the establishment of church schools, education, and the publication of western European books. In January 1728, he moved from St. Petersburg to Moscow when the royal court transferred to the old capital.

The next two years in Moscow were difficult ones for Archbishop Theofan. Now that Peter the Great had died, a group within the Church tried to destroy the Synod and re-establish the Patriarchate, in order to make the Church independent of Government control.[25] These individuals, in 1728, published a tract entitled *Rock of Faith,* written by the late President of the Synod, Metropolitan Stefan Iavorskii. Although Iavorskii had been a reformer in the first two decades, when President of the Synod, he began to oppose the "Protestantization" of the Orthodoxy. His *Rock of Faith,* as indicated by its very title, is a disguised diatribe against Peter the Great's policies. This group soon won influence among the members of the Privy Council because many envisioned Theofan as Peter's successor in his desires to continue the reform work.[26] No doubt, Theofan was particularly embittered by this struggle, not only because he was a churchman, but because he himself had given birth to the Holy Synod.

Theofan, however, found comfort among others, such as Tatishchev, who shared his ambitions. He quickly won the respect of his colleague Kondoides' former pupil, Prince Antoikh Kantemir, with whom he exchanged satires during these years. In his first poem, "Theofan Archbishop of Novgorod 'to the author of the satire,'" he encouraged his young friend to continue his pursuit of knowledge, and sounded the hope that the Learned Guard would lead the Russian people from the "evils of ignorance" to the "fruit of knowledge."[27] Theofan also associated with the members of the Russian Academy who were in Moscow at that time. Many made use of his extensive library, which contained over 3,000 volumes, and his home became the first "salon" in Russia.

During the succession crisis of 1730, Theofan played an instrumental role in retaining autocracy in Russia.[28] Shortly thereafter, he regained a leading place in Church affairs. He died on 8 September 1736.

Theofan's young admirer, Prince Antiokh Dmitrievich Kantemir, was born on 21 September 1709 in Moldavia.[29] His family had been the ruling house of the principality until they escaped to Russia when Antiokh was three years old. It seems that his father, Prince Dmitrii, had concluded a secret agreement with Peter the Great in 1711, asking him to liberate the principalities from Turkish rule during the Pruth Campaign. When the Campaign failed, the Kantemir family joined the Russian camp rather than fall prey to the Turks. Prince Dmitrii spent the remainder of his life in the Russian service.

As hospodars of Moldavia, the Kantemir family always had the opportunity to receive a good education. Prince Dmitrii had studied medicine, philology, philosophy, and music in Greece and Constantinople before becoming Hospodar in 1710. Later, he wrote a four-volume history of Turkey, and Peter the Great valued Prince Dmitrii's erudition so highly that he considered him a candidate for the first presidency of the proposed Academy of Sciences.

Prince Dmitrii saw that his son Antiokh received the best education possible in Russia. His Greek tutor, Anastasii Kondoides, accompanied the family to Russia.[30] His other tutor, I. I. Il'inskii, was a recognized poet and translator. Later, the young Prince studied at the Moscow Slavic-Greek-Latin Academy, and, in the mid-1720's, enrolled in the university established with the Academy of Sciences. During the next six years, in St. Petersburg and in Moscow, he studied physics under Daniel Bernoulli and Georg Bülffinger, history under Gottlieb von Bayer, philosophy under Friedrich Gross, and mathematics under Friedrich Mayer of Tubingen. It was Gross, his favorite professor, who introduced Kantemir to the writings of the European philosophers. Samuel Pufendorf's *Einleitung in die Historie der vornehmsten Europäschen Staaten* had been translated into Russian in 1718, and his *De Officio Hominis et Civis Juxta Legem Naturalem Libri Duo* in 1726. Gross used the latter as a text for his students. Kantemir also studied the political ideas of Jacques Benigne Bossuet, whose *Histoire Universelle* was a long defense of absolutism.

Although Kantemir was only in his teens when he studied under Gross, he already evidenced abilities of genius. In 1729, he wrote a satire, "On the Abuse of Learning," which he sent anonymously to Archbishop Theofan.[31] The poem was a gesture of support for Theofan's position against the followers of Iavorskii. Later, he wrote another satire, "On the Envy and Greed of the Malicious Nobility," which was a diatribe against the plots of Menshikov and his kind.[32] There can be no doubt that young Prince Kantemir shared the reform spirit of Theofan and Tatishchev, as evidenced in his euology to Peter the Great, "Peter," written in early 1730.[33] Kantemir's literary achievements were not limited to

31

poetry; in that same year, 1730, he completed a Russian translation of Fontenelle's *Entretiens sur la pluralité des mondes.*[34]

Kantemir was also active in Russian politics. When a student of Gross, he was commissioned lieutenant in the Preobrazhenskii guard regiment, and he wrote the proclamation bestowing autocratic powers on Anne during the succession crisis of 1730.[35] Two years later, in 1732, he was appointed Ambassador to London. When in England, he read extensively in the works of More, Newton, Locke, Hobbes, Milton, Pope, Swift, and Addison and Steele.[36] In September 1738, he was appointed Ambassador to Paris.

When in Paris, Kantemir sought out the President of the Académie Française, Montesquieu.[37] No doubt, Kantemir was interested in meeting Montesquieu because he had translated the Frenchman's *Lettres Persannes* into Russian. Moreover, part of Kantemir's commission was to establish a link between the Russian and French Academies. Kantemir impressed Montesquieu more by erudition than by charm, since the Frenchman found his Russian friend very cold and austere. Moreover, it seems that Montesquieu took offense at Kantemir's admiration for Bossuet. This is understandable since Kantemir, like Bossuet, was a supporter of absolutism, and Montesquieu wrote his *Lettres Persannes* specifically as an attack against the ideas of the Bishop of Meaux. Nevertheless, Kantemir seems to have exercised some influence on Montesquieu. Robert Shackleton believes that from conversations with Kantemir, Montesquieu derived his knowledge of Russia which he used in his major work, *L'Esprit des Lois.*[38]

In 1744, Kantemir traveled to Italy for his health.[39] He died in Paris on 11 April of the same year at the age of 35.

After his return from Sweden, Tatishchev remained until fall 1727 in St. Petersburg, where he spent most of his time working on historical sources[40] in preparation for his *Russian History.* In September, an imperial decree ordered him and Count Platon Musin-Pushkin to travel to Moscow to administer a currency reform.[41] The decree established a new five-kopek piece and called for the use of silver in the monetary system. No doubt, Tatishchev's experience in Sweden was the basis for his being assigned to the post of Currency Controller.

In Moscow, Tatishchev had the opportunity to associate and work with his former instructor and friend Jacob Bruce, who had resided there since the death of Peter the Great.[42] Through Bruce, Tatishchev associated with the members of the Academy who were living there. He met Christian Goldbach, Secretary of the Academy; the natural philosopher David Messerschmidt; and the moral philosopher Friedrich Gross, who was tutor to Emperor Peter II and Prince Kantemir. Through Gross, he was introduced to Georg Bernhard Bülffinger, who had been a student of the German philosopher Christian Wolff and who had an extraordinary knowledge of European philosophical systems.

Tatishchev devoted almost all of his time to intellectual pursuits during these years. It is known that he frequented the library of Prince D. M. Golitsyn, even though he was not on the best of terms with the Privy Councilor.[43] Much to Tatishchev's interest, Golitsyn's library contained an incomplete manuscript translation of Pufendorf's *De Jure Naturae et Gentium Libri Octo*. He also used the library of his friend Theofan Prokopovich; and, with both libraries combined, he had over 6,000 volumes at his disposal. Tatishchev, to be sure, did not neglect his work in history. During this time, he read Pufendorf's *Einleitung in die Historie der vornehmsten Europäschen Staaten* and helped Bayer work on Russian chronicles.[44]

It was entirely natural that, after Peter's death, Tatishchev sought the company of those who supported the westernization of Russia. The discussions with Archbishop Theofan, Prince Kantemir, and members of the Academy brought the world of the Western European Enlightenment to Russia. Their society gave Tatishchev the opportunity to absorb and discuss in depth philosophical ideas of his time with the most learned men in Russia. His interest in Russian history well suited the temperament of his friends.

The Learned Guard, however, did not exactly withdraw into a strictly intellectual world. The were acutely aware of the political situation, and they seem to have discussed it at great length. Indeed, Tatishchev and Archbishop Theofan had participated directly in the progress and reform work of Peter's reign, and now they saw their own projects decaying during the rule of Menshikov and the princes Dolgorukii. The Learned Guard's enmity for the "aristocratic" party no doubt was reflected in the satires written by Prince Kantemir. They wanted the return of a powerful sovereign who would restore the pace of reform.

33

Chapter V

The Succession Crisis of 1730

The Learned Guard unexpectedly influenced the affairs of Russia during the succession crisis of 1730. When the members of the nobility began to challenge the authority of the Supreme Privy Council, V. N. Tatishchev submitted a project which proposed the Learned Guard's ideas as a solution to Russia's problems. His project, however, was rejected when the various factions of the nobility saw that they could wrench certain concessions from the Council which would suit their particular class interests. When it appeared that the Council had all but silenced opposition to its rule, the Learned Guard and their supporters conspired to bring about a palace revolution to restore autocracy in Russia.

The succession crisis of 1730 began on 19 January, when the 15-year-old Emperor Peter II died of smallpox on his wedding day.[1] The situation was particularly difficult because the boy Emperor had neglected to designate an heir to the throne in accord with Peter the Great's decree of February 1722.

Immediately following the boy Emperor's death, Princes V. V. and M. V. Dolgorukii and Prince D. M. Golitsyn joined forces with the members of the Privy Council to decide on a method of succession. They first ignored Prince A. G. Dolgorukii's claim that his daughter Catherine, who had been affianced to Peter, had a legitimate right to the throne. Almost as quickly, they rejected Empress Catherine's "testament," which designated her eldest illegitimate daughter as legal heir. The members then turned to the daughters of Peter the Great's brother and co-Tsar, Ivan V. They rejected the eldest, Catherine of Mecklenburg, because of her German husband. The younger Anne of Courland, however, was most acceptable because she was husbandless and submissive. The youngest, Praskovie, seems not to have been considered.

Later in the morning of the 19th, the Privy Council held a meeting in the Kremlin to announce its decision to the Senate and Synod and to high officials and members of the nobility. It was at this time that Prince D. M. Golitsyn explained that Anne must agree to eight "Conditions" before she could come to Moscow.[2] In short, Anne would have to obtain the consent of the existing Privy Council before she could start

34

war, conclude peace, impose new taxes, make important appointments in both civil and military administrations, "deprive the nobility of life, property, and honour without trial," grant estates and villages, make promotions to court offices, and spend state revenues. Though not stated in the Conditions, Anne had to promise not to bring her lover, Ernst Johann Biron, to Russia. That same day, Prince V. L. Dolgorukii left for Mitau in Courland to orer the Russian throne and to present the Conditions to Anne.

In spite of the Council's efforts to prevent news of the Conditions from reaching Anne before Dolgorukii's presentation, Iaguzhinskii, Archbishop Theofan Prokopovich, and the German adventurer Reinhold Löwenwolde sent emissaries to Mitau. Their motive was to find a way to bring about abandonment of the Conditions and the rule by the Privy Council, and to retain the autocratic monarchy. In a word, Iaguzhinskii instructed Anne to accept the Conditions and anything else that the Privy Council required of her. He then tsked her to trust him because, in the meanwhile, ". . . he would use his best endeavours to increase the party of such as were not at all pleased at this government by the council of state, . . . and that after the arrival of her Majesty everything would be terminated to her wish."[3] Anne accepted all the Conditions on 28 January; Dolgorukii returned to Moscow with the news five days later.

Because of the growing criticism of the Conditions, the Privy Council invited members of the nobility to present their own reform plans, which in turn would be submitted to Anne upon her arrival. The 12 known projects are usually divided into two groups: those which represent the opinions of the Generality and those of the rank-and-file nobility (gentry or lower nobility).

The ideas of the Generality can be understood from a 12-point project submitted by M. A. Matiushkin.[4] Opposing the oligarchic character of Golitsyn's Conditions, Matiushkin recommended that the present Privy Council be expanded to 12 members, and that the Generality and other nobles concur with the Council for important decisions. Although he suggested that the Senate be expanded to 11 members, he left it in charge only of administrative matters. Only one member from each family could serve in the Senate.

Just as Golitsyn's Conditions forbade Anne from ruling autocratically, Matiushkin's project contained a general provision that she would have to obtain the consent of the Council and nobility before making laws concerning State administration and "the common weal." Characteristically, the project protected the nobility from Peter the Great's practice of forcing them to serve as artisans or sailors. Promotion was to be based on duration of service, and the Government was asked to satisfy the complaints of the various classes in accord with their social status. Matiushkin and his supporters asked for estate inheritance laws and petitioned—symbolically—that the capital be returned to Moscow.

On 7 February, the rank-and-file nobles submitted a project which provided for a "High Government" of 21 persons and a Senate of 11 (100 in a variant).[5] No more than two members of a particular family could be candidates for the High Government. All important statutes had to be drafted and consented to by the High Government, the Senate, and the nobility. The rank-and-file nobility also requested that a better service system be planned, wherein they would not have to serve as sailors or artisans and they could retire after 25 years. At the same time, they asked for a system of military promotions and laws concerning estate inheritances, and suggested improvement in conditions for merchants and peasants.

From the date included in his concluding remarks, V. N. Tatishchev was one of the first to present a plan for reform. As mentioned in the document, the ideas were discussed among several members of the nobility on 4 February at the house of V. Ia. Novosiltsev. As published in the journal *Utro*, Tatishchev's "Unrestrained and Concerted Discourse and Opinion of the Assembled Russian Gentry on State Government"[6] can be divided into four parts: first, an introduction which poses four questions concerning the foundation of government in Russia; second, a "discourse" or historical essay to answer the introductory questions; third, ten recommendations to help Anne govern Russia; and, fourth, a summary of events leading to the Empress' assuming autocratic rule.

Tatishchev characteristically began his project with an explanation that a ruler should be chosen by his subjects according to natural law.[7] He warned that, if this law were not observed, Russia would suffer grave consequences similar to the ones experienced during the reigns of Boris Godunov and Vasilii Shuiskii. He unequivocally stated that a ruling aristocracy would bring even greater diseasters, since Government leadership then could not be "single-minded." At this point, he posed four questions relative to the succession crisis: First, at the end of an "inherited" government, who has the power to rule over the people? Second, to whom does legislative power belong? Third, if a single-rule government (monarchy) must be changed, which form of government is proper for the customs and situation of the nation? And, fourth, how is that government established?

In the second part of the document, i.e., the "discourse," Tatishchev answered these questions by using examples from history and his own political theory as derived from natural law. In response to the first question, he said that all loyalty to a government is released at the end of a hereditary monarchy. For the second, he emphasized that all laws originate from the ruler or, citing the example of the consulship in ancient Rome, from anyone to whom the ruler delegates that power. In answer to which form of government was best for Russia, Tatishchev presented an essay which placed the problem in geographical and historical perspective.

Tatishchev began his analysis with reference to Aristotle's three forms of government: (1) monarchy, or single rule; (2) aristocracy, or select rule; and (3) democracy, or common rule. He first said that democracy is good only where the region is safe from foreign invasion and, assuming that the state is small in size, where everyone is able to congregate to make decisions. Moreover, the people of a democracy must be "enlightened" and have respect for law. He also recognized that mixtures of these types can occur: a monarchic aristocracy in Germany and Poland, and characteristics of all three in England and Sweden. For Russia, however, as for Spain, France, Persia, Turkey, India, and China, he thought that only an autocracy (monarchy)[8] was feasible. In reference to the problems of ruling a large state, he pointed out that even in ancient Rome, where there was an emperor ruling with an aristocracy and democracy, an individual had to assume autocratic powers in times of war.

Considering Russia's own historical perspective, he thought that monarchy was the most suitable form. He reasoned that, from the time of Riurik, and, even earlier, with the Scythians, there had always been single rule in Russia; and, under monarchy, the country prospered no less than did the other European nations. Mstislav the Great's successors, however, refused to obey the Grand Prince, and the country consequently weakened under the divided rule. Russia then suffered Tatar and Lithuanian invasions for 200 years. Ivan the Great restored the monarchy and destroyed the aristocracy, and Russian prospered until the reign of Boris Godunov. Under false Dmitrii, the country became politically aimless, thereby permitting the Swedes and Poles to occupy the borderlands. Since the election of Michael Romanov, who was chosen according to the precepts of natural law, the borderlands had been returned and Russia had grown in wealth, especially under Peter the Great.

In accord with this historical perspective and the natural law, Tatishchev then listed several principles concerning the relationship of Russian subjects to their ruler.[9] First, the ruler should have advisors; and, if he does not accept their "wisdom," then he is liable to God's punishment.[10] Second, his authority must be enforced everywhere in the State, and the nobles must support him. In the same sense, foreign nations must also respect the State's (ruler's) dignity. Third, the State must be aware of opportunists or intriguers, as did ancient Rome and Greece; but, at the same time, not become fanatic in doing away with favorites, as Russia did during the reign of Ivan IV. And, fourth, a Privy Council should be established in the Roman tradition, in order to provide "security" for the monarch.

After having presented these general principles for government in Russia, Tatishchev felt that Anne's reign called for more specific recommendations. He thought that, even though Anne had ruled well in Courland, her lack of knowledge of Russian laws (and customs) and her being a woman would handicap decisive leadership. Therefore, until the Almighty provided for a male person to assume the throne, Tatishchev proposed a 10-point project. First of all, a Supreme Ruling Senate of 21 should absorb the Privy Council. Another body of 100, chosen for three years and divided into three separate groups, should administer economic and similar matters and meet together in the event of national emergency. Tatishchev also provided for elective process to fill vacancies; but, in order to guarantee against oligarchy, he limited participation in both groups to only one member per family. At the same time, he advocated a system of police or "overseers" to discourage and prevent intrigue by opportunists. He also proposed that Russian laws be codified. Peter the Great's demands on the nobility were retained and even extended, for Tatishchev wanted them to serve in the military during youth, and gave them the responsibility of "enlightening" the nation. He also suggested that the clergy be responsible for education in rural areas, and that commerce be encouraged by removing the restrictions on merchants. Finally, to avoid future succession problems, he proposed that an *ulozhenie* define a method for the transfer of authority from one ruler to another. Thirty-seven signatures immediately follow on the document, including those of S. A. Saltykov and Prince A. M. Cherkasskii. Tatishchev related that over 300 signed other copies.

In his summary of events, i.e., the fourth part of the document, Tatishchev explained that, on the 23rd,[11] he and several others gathered at the house of Lieutenant-General Prince Bariatinskii and agreed to abolish the Supreme Privy Council and to preserve the autocracy. Tatischev and some others then went to Cherkasskii's home, where they asked Prince A. D. Kantemir to draft a proclamation requesting Anne to assume autocratic power. Seventy-four signed the document at Bariatinskii's, and another 93 when they returned to Cherkasskii's residence. At the same time, messengers were sent to the palace guard regiments, where 58 officers and 37 cavalry guards signed. That same evening, they informed Anne of their intentions.

On 25 February, Prince Cherkasskii and G. P. Chernyshev led 150 soldiers to the Kremlin and demanded an audience with Anne.[12] It was at this point that Tatishchev read a petition which has become known as the "Cherkasskii Project."[13] In this declaration, they suggested that "the majority of the people" were not in agreement with Golitsyn's Conditions and said that the Supreme Privy Council had refused to consider several of the reform plans presented to it. In order to rectify this situation, they asked Anne to approve of an assembly of representatives from the families of all high officials and noblemen, which would examine all the reform plans and submit one for her approval.

Anne was startled. She had expected them to present a proclamation giving her autocratic power. When the nobles left the room, however, the guards began to press for a return to autocratic rule. The nobles reassembled, after which Tatishchev presented a project, drafted by Kantemir, which conferred upon Anne the powers that she had expected.[14] At the same time, they "begged" her to establish a 21-member Ruling Senate in place of the High Senate and Privy Council, and to consider an "administration" subject to her future approval. Most characteristically, the petitioners referred to themselves as her "Imperial Majesty's most humble servants."[15] Anne thereupon tore up the Conditions, after confronting Golitsyn with the charge that they were not in accord with the demands of the nation. She then promised to rule with the counsels of a Senate ". . . composed of persons of the greatest experience and the most acknowledged probity. . . ."[16] On 25 February 1730, the Supreme Privy Council was abolished, and the nobles' demands were left unanswered. Empress Anne now ruled as well as reigned over Russia.

For over a century, historians such as N. A. Popov,[17] D. M. Korsakov,[18] and Marc Raeff[19] have referred to Tatishchev's project as an example of the lower nobility's views, because several members of that class signed the document. Recently, however, the Soviet scholar G. A. Protasov discovered that Tatishchev wrote the first, second, and fourth parts of the document sometime after 1730.[20] According to Protasov, "The project does not appear to be a document of the actions of the *dvorianstvo* [nobility] during the events of 1730; it is the result of the later understanding of the author's notes on the *dvorianstvo's* plans in the period."[21] The opinions expressed in the "discourse," therefore, were Tatishchev's own and cannot be associated with those of the nobility. The 10 points, however, were written during the crisis, and they are reflected in the other projects submitted at that time. Because of this time lapse, Protasov concluded that Tatishchev wrote the other parts to justify his activities in 1730 with political theories developed at a later date.

From a comparison of the various projects, it appears that Protasov was correct in concluding that Tatishchev's does not represent the view of the lower nobility or the nobility in general. The most obvious point is that Tatishchev did not make any restrictions whatsoever on the autocracy. In fact, he insisted that only the monarch have legislative powers, although he did recognize the need for assemblies to counsel the ruler and help in administration. He also reaffirmed the nobility's obligation to serve in the military; and, at the same time, assigned to them the task of advancing Russia intellectually. Moreover, Tatishchev's provision for the codification of Russian laws and a declaration of the need for an *ulozhenie* to solve the succession problem make his the only project which took the real problems of Russian government into consideration. The whole tone of his document differs from that of the others: Whereas the plans of the rank-and-file nobility, Generality, and Supreme Privy Council appear to make demands and try to secure certain prerogatives or guarantees from the monarch, Tatishchev's is more concerned with strengthening the Russian State by making everyone function in the service of a wise and absolute monarch. In a word, the nobles as a whole wanted to slow down the pace of modernization, or even return to their Muscovite-pre-Petrine privileges; Tatishchev and his party wanted to continue the "enlightenment" and reforms of Peter the Great.

The "discourse" or historical essay may have been written after the event, as Protasov discovered; but his claim that Tatishchev wrote it to justify his activities in 1730 lacks sufficient evidence. Tatishchev thought of all the ideas incorporated into his project long before the succession crisis occurred. First of all, he had been a student of reform plans for Russia since the early 1720's. In fact, Peter the Great had sent him to Sweden in 1724 to study other administrations with the intention of introducing the same into Russia. Furthermore, Tatishchev had played active roles in Government as a State factory administrator in the reign of Peter the Great, and as Currency Controller under Peter II. No doubt, too, he was well acquainted with the problems of indecisive monarchical leadership, or court intrigues, and of a host of other similar difficulties which plagued Russia. As a former loyal supporter of Peter the Great, Tatishchev identified himself with westernization and kept in mind what was necessary to re-establish a reform-minded Government in Russia.

The same argument holds for the theoretical sections of his document. After Peter the Great's death, Tatishchev devoted most of his time to studying Russian history. He also acquainted himself with the most advanced political theories of the Western European Enlightenment, and he discussed these ideas with his friends Archbishop Theofan Prokopovich and Prince A. D. Kantemir. Moreover, the "Learned Guard," as the three referred to themselves, had the expressed intention of ridding the Government of intriguers and of restoring the progress and reform work experienced under Peter the Great. Through their study of political theory and Russian history, they reasoned that their country needed an absolute and wise monarch. Therefore, Tatishchev merely recorded or added his opinions to the document as an explanation, rather than justification, of his activities in 1730. Without a doubt, the ideas contained in the essay were in tune with the 10 points which Protasov assured were written during the crisis.

In all probability, some of the nobles signed Tatishchev's project because it was the first one submitted for their approval and seemed to provide a solution to Russia's problems. As the crisis continued, however, the nobility realized that they could wrench concessions from the Privy Council and Empress Anne and, therefore, drew up other plans which modified Tatishchev's ideas to suit their own interests.

Rather than representing the opinions of the lower nobility, Tatishchev's project reflected the views of the Learned Guard and their supporters, individuals who rose to prominence through their personal services to Peter the Great and who wished to restore his reform work in Russia. Right from the outset, when the Privy Council imposed the Conditions on Anne, they worked collectively and individually to retain the autocracy. Tatishchev, for his part, tried to persuade the nobles to support his project by sharing with them the ideas he had discussed with his friends over the previous three years. His efforts, however, failed when the Generality and other nobles used the reform plans to limit the autocracy and to secure guarantees for their own class interests.

On the evening of 24 February, the Learned Guard and several others resolved that the only way to preserve Russia was to bring about a palace revolution. In all likelihood, they obtained the support of the nobles by suggesting that they join in presenting a declaration to Anne expressing their grievances against the Privy Council. Just when the Council and Anne yielded to their demands, the palace guard—by agreement with the Learned Guard—demanded that Anne receive autocratic powers. This was the impetus which was necessary for the conspirators to gain the assent of the other nobles. It was at this point that they presented Prince Kantemir's declaration and restored absolutism in Russia.

Although Tatishchev's "Undestrained and Concerted Discourse" has importance as a document of the ideas and program of the Learned

Guard, it has an even greater value as a landmark of eighteenth century political thought and Russian cultural history.[22] In the "Discourse," Tatishchev treated history and politics as natural sciences, similarly to the way that Newton carried on his investigations in physics. In short, Tatishchev used the experience of geography and Russian history to construct a proper form of government for Russia. This method, induction, evidenced a distinct departure on Tatishchev's part from the seventeenth century practice of deduction, which placed all historical phenomena within an *à priori* system. Although Tatishchev referred to natural law theory, his main argument for the acceptance of his project rested upon his analysis of Russian history. In this sense, Tatishchev's document serves as a bridge between the methods of such seventeenth century philosophers as Descartes and Leibniz and the eighteenth century philosopher Montesquieu.

In the social sciences, Montesquieu's *L'Esprit des Lois* has often been regarded as the first important attempt at constructing a general system or principle from analysis of particular, observable phenomena. Nevertheless, V. N. Tatishchev's "Discourse" had uséd this same method clearly four years before the French scholar undertook his work. Moreover, although there are great similarities to their conclusions, Tatishchev's argument that geography (in the sense of natural boundaries and space, logistics) and history influence the type of government which a country should have seems to have greater validity than Montesquieu's climatic factors.[23] Montesquieu, to be sure, examined these factors—and others which Tatishchev neglected because of the particular circumstances of his document—but Tatishchev was far more clear on these particular points. In fact, there is a high probability that Montesquieu knew of Tatishchev's ideas. Kantemir visited Montesquieu in 1738, precisely at the time when the French philosopher was preparing his notebooks for *L'Esprit des Lois*. Montesquieu began his research on the work in late 1734 and finished the final draft in 1747.[24] If nothing else, the similarity of methods and content demonstrates that, on certain questions, Tatishchev or the Learned Guard was in tune with, perhaps even ahead of, the most advanced thinkers of western Europe.

In other respects, too, the Learned Guard shared the intellectual temperament of their western contemporaries. They possessed a distinct faith in, and wanted to restore, the progress of the Enlightenment in Russia. During the years that they were removed from influential positions near the throne, they made a dogma of spreading learning and reason in Russia. Earlier, in his Ecclesiastical Regulation, Archbishop Theofan had insisted on a rounded education for clergymen, and he did his utmost to promulgate western ideas in Russia. Tatishchev advocated a system of elementary education, and in his project he assigned to the nobility the task of "Enlightening" the nation. And Kantemir, for his part, voiced disdain for ignorance in his satires. In short, the Learned Guard believed in the "immutability of reason," that they could transform Russian society and politics by promulgating the "fruits of knowledge."

Perhaps the major indication that the Learned Guard were forerunners of eighteenth century thought was that they played an active role in society and politics.[25] Both Tatishchev and Archbishop Theofan aided Peter the Great in the work of reform. In the 1720's, they had the explicit desire to continue the Petrine tradition, precisely because it rationalized government and society. And, during the succession crisis of 1730, they were not content merely to philosophize about government like their seventeenth century western predecessors; they worked together to realize their ideas by restoring autocracy, an "enlightened absolutism," in Russia.

Chapter VI

Years of Disgrace

Following the succession crisis of 1730, V. N. Tatishchev continued to serve in the mint. That April, he was chosen Master of Ceremonies for Empress Anne's coronation pageant.[1] He organized the various processions and introduced State officials and foreign ambassadors to the new Empress. In the summer of 1731, he arranged the transfer of the court to St. Petersburg when Empress Anne wanted to return to the new capital.

Shortly thereafter, Empress Anne's consort, Ernst Johann Biron [Bühren], and Count M. G. Golovkin accused Tatishchev, and others identified as Zybin, Neronov, and Mokeev, of embezzlement.[2] According to Biron's account, they formed a private purchasing company to acquire coins from the mint at a price below the official values. Biron also accused Tatishchev of paying a promissory note of 4,200 rubles with State funds.

Tatishchev admitted several years later that he had illegally exchanged coins through a private company.[3] He defended his activity by explaining that he considered the profit made in the exchanges as compensation for a salary which he never received. Moreover, he sold the company coins damaged in the stamping process; these coins were of no use to the State anyway. Nevertheless, Tatishchev was subsequently dismissed from State service.

Tatishchev's removal from State service was a traumatic experience for him. Over the past 17 years, he had come to identify himself with his duties and loyalty to Government service. Moreover, his former friends in the nobility now shunned him for advocating preservation of the autocracy and for supporting Petrine service obligations in 1730. No doubt, during the next few years, he reflected upon his former role in State service. Perhaps even more important, he gave much thought to the general problems which Russia, and particularly the nobility, faced in the years after the Petrine reforms.

Tatishchev included many of these reflections in a dialogue, "A Conversation of Two Friends on the Use of Knowledge and Education,"[4] which he based upon a discussion held sometime in 1731 or 1732 among Princes S. G. Dolgorukii and A. D. Kantemir, Archbishop Theofan

Prokopovich, and several members of the Academy of Sciences. N. A. Popov, who edited the "Conversation" in the late 1880's, found four manuscripts of the work. According to his analysis, Tatishchev wrote the major part of the "Conversation" in 1733. The manuscript which Popov used in his edition contained 120 questions and answers.

Tatishchev opened his "Conversation" by explaining that learning demands reason in the same way that ability requires skill. All knowledge, he wrote, emanates from human nature; and, therefore, "The proper study of man is man." One must know himself to choose his role in life, and reason correctly to recognize good and to avoid evil. Much in tune with contemporary European philosophy, Tatishchev defined good as man's using reason to seek truth, well-being, and pleasure.

In describing man's reasoning process, Tatishchev explained that, according to Cicero, Newton, and Leibniz, man is composed of both body and soul. Man's intellectual powers reside in the soul, which memorizes, conjectures, and judges from information obtained through the body's five senses. Man reasons when his soul or mind reflects upon something, and his will chooses when the reflecting process finishes. The will can choose between good and evil, or well-being and misfortune. The will is usually motivated by man's quest for honor, desires of the flesh, and fulfillment of the teachings of God.

A person's motivations change with age. During youth, a man is motivated by material things and desires of the flesh. In manhood, he possesses a clearer perspective on life, fulfills the ambitions of youth, and lives either honorably or dishonorably. In old age, a person usually follows the teachings of the Church, and acquires an inner peace. One can also possess the characteristics of old age as the result of a serious illness.

Mankind, Tatishchev wrote, increases its knowledge similarly to the way an individual matures. The first landmark in civilization's progress was the use of writing. Since the time of the early Egyptians, man has been able to preserve knowledge in written form for future generations. The second important event was the birth of Christ. Christ taught man kindness and what Tatishchev called "moral love [moral'no liubve]." The most recent stage in man's progress was the invention of printing. Movable type quickened the spread of knowledge. Tatishchev was apparently aware of the seventeenth century "battle of the ancients and moderns." He noted that, in ancient times, philosophers spoke of a "golden age" when humanity would live without vexation. Contemporary philosophers, he wrote, believe that "This is the best of all possible worlds."

When asked which philosophers were the most important to study,

Tatishchev referred to many important ones in the European cultural tradition. He noted that Pythagoras was the first philosopher, and that he was famous for his studies in theology, jurisprudence, and astronomy, as well as his mathematical observations. Tatishchev also cited Aristotle, Plato, Socrates, Draco, Augustine, Tertulian, Seneca, and the Roman historian Tacitus. He also recommended the writings of Descartes, Copernicus, Galileo, Pufendorf, and Hugo Grotius for an understanding of modern philosophy and science. One should also study theologians, Tatishchev wrote, especially since Peter the Great had given to the Church the task of teaching love of God. Christ Himself was the most important, after which Tatishchev suggested Pope Gregory the Great, Origen, and Dionysius the Areopagite. He also referred to St. Ignatius, John Wycliffe, and Jan Hus among more contemporary theologians.

Tatishchev had a utilitarian outlook towards education, and he categorized subject matter according to its usefulness: 1. necessary, 2. useful, 3. foppish or amusing [*shchegol'skaia ili uveselia iushchaia*], 4. curious or vain [*liubopytnyia ili tshchetnyia*], and 5. harmful. According to Tatishchev's classification, it is necessary for everyone to learn to speak and to know the laws of Church and State. Writing, geography, and history, as well as rhetoric and knowledge of foreign languages, are most useful for those in State service. Tatishchev considered dancing, music, painting, and poetry "foppish," since they are cultivated chiefly by courtiers. Astrology and alchemy were "futile," in Tatishchev's opinion, because "they contain little truth."

Tatishchev devoted the second half of the "Conversation" to a discussion of some of the problems plaguing Russia at that time. The most serious problem to him was Russia's lack of an educational system. Although he praised Peter the Great for founding the Academy of Sciences, he regretted that Russia did not have a school system to prepare students for entry into the university attached to it. He compared the situation to that of a man who constructs a mill without providing for water to turn it. In Tatishchev's time, the gentry were educated at home by their parents, a condition which he thought was undesirable, or they studied in western Europe. In short, Tatishchev wanted Russia to develop an adequate educational system. He recommended that the Government establish schools in each town; train teachers in foreign languages and modern science; and encourage the printing of books on mathematics, history, and geography in the Russian language. He particularly liked the program of the Moscow Slavic-Greek-Latin Academy, because it included rhetoric and the study of the Latin classics. Nevertheless, he thought that the writings of Malebranche, Descartes, Pufendorf, and other moderns should be added to complete the curriculum.

Tatishchev also wanted Russia to develop its own educational heritage similar to that of England and France. He credited the absolute monarchs King Henry VIII and Queen Elizabeth of England, and Kings Henry IV and Louis XIV of France for supporting the arts and sciences in those countries. He claimed that the greatest freedom existed in their reigns because the growth of knowledge spreads truth, which, in turn, frees man from ignorance and superstition. Education was particularly important for teaching Russians respect for law and the Government, since Tatishchev attributed the seventeenth century revolts of Bolotnikov and Razin to the ignorance of the population.[5]

In Tatishchev's analysis, education was of greatest importance to the Russian gentry. He suggested that Russia establish schools for its nobility similar to those in England and France. The nobility could then study geography, history, and foreign languages in preparation for careers in the military and in the new civil service. Through education, the nobility could resume their traditional role in Government service, and fulfill the new demands on their class made by Peter the Great. Tatishchev hoped that the Russian nobility would become an élite class and bring western European cultural traditions and knowledge to Russia. No doubt, he had this idea in mind when he assigned to the nobility the task of "enlightening" Russia in his "Unrestrained and Concerted Discourse and Opinion of the Assembled Russian Gentry on State Government" in 1730.[6]

In his discussion of politics, Tatishchev reiterated some of the arguments posed in his "Unrestrained and Concerted Discourse," and emphasized that monarchy was the most suitable form of government for Russia. He defined politics as the wisdom of governing a state rationally and in accord with natural law. In international relations, natural law required states to respect and assist each other in solving mutual problems.

Politics led Tatishchev to the topic of jurisprudence. Perhaps suggesting a comparison to western Europe, he observed that Russia had a long tradition of written law. He claimed that a written code existed at the the time of Riurik in the ninth century, and he referred to the *Russkaia Pravda*[7] of Iaroslav the Wise and the *Sudebnik* of Ivan IV.[8] Only the monarch could legislate in an autocracy. Tatishchev noted, however, that the monarch had to consider the state's customs and traditions in making decrees. He then pointed out that Russia's laws were in disorder; and he recommended, as he did in his "Unrestrained and Concerted Discourse," that the Government formulate a new code. At the same time, he ex-

47

pressed the hope that Empress Anne would continue the reforms of Peter the Great.

Tatishchev closed the "Conversation" by reaffirming the usefulness of knowledge and learning, and by assuring his readers of the benefits of education.

No doubt, Tatishchev's dismissal from civil service caused him to reflect upon Russia's political and social difficulties at that time. Although he possessed the outlook of the new Petrine civil servant, he noticed that the nobility in general, the class which Peter the Great intended for his new civil service, did not. They had not completely developed a new mentality within the first years after Peter's death. Their society was in turmoil to some degree after the Petrine revolution, and they were slowly adjusting to their new conditions and service obligations.

Tatishchev thought that a good part of this problem was due to the nobility's lack of education in preparation for their new tasks. Russia simply did not have an educational system to provide them with the necessary training for State service. At the same time, Tatishchev saw that education would have a greater importance for the nobility as a class. Through education, by carrying western European ideas to Russia, the Russian nobleman would see himself as part of a new élite. He would possess a new identity, and resume in a new way his traditional social importance within the Petrine system.

The Russian nobility followed Tatishchev's formula within the next few decades. By the second half of the eighteenth century, noblemen assumed the rule of *Kulturträger* and brought western culture and education to Russia.[9] They came to identify themselves in society and in Government service as the new Petrine élite. Of course, that is not to say that Tatishchev as an individual exercised a direct influence in creating their new identity. He merely absorbed and reflected the mentality created by the new civil service more rapidly than others. It is important, however, that he posed a solution to the problem which, to a considerable extent, was appropriately demonstrated in the years ahead.

Chapter VII

Tatishchev's Urals "Empire"

In March 1734, V. N. Tatishchev resumed his activities in State service when the Commerce College assigned him to administer the Urals State factory system. During the next three years in Ekaterinburg, he attempted to reform the factory administration by enforcing standards and techniques which he had studied in Sweden. More important, Tatishchev used this opportunity to create out of the Urals industrial complex an administration and society which reflected the spirit of the Petrine era.

Early in 1733, a Senate committee sponsored an investigation of the Urals metal industry.[1] Georg Hennin, Tatishchev's successor in Ekaterinburg, had encountered numerous difficulties in administering the Urals factory system and requested to be relieved of his post. Production dropped in the early 1730's, and Konstantin Gordeev, Secretary of the Mining Office of the Commerce College, sent officials to the Urals to investigate the situation.[2] In the spring, the Senate established two committees to study the feasibility of leasing the State factories to private entrepreneurs as a means of increasing production.

One committee, headed by Baron P. P. Shafirov, investigated the potential revenue which would be acquired by the leasings. The other, formed by Count M. G. Golovkin, had to decide the question of placing the factories under private management. Almost a year later, on 17 March 1734, the Golovkin committee decided to retain State management of the factories, and appointed Tatishchev to reform the administration and find ways to increase production. On or before 23 March, Tatishchev helped draft an "Instruction" which outlined his new duties.[3]

The Instruction ordered Tatishchev to increase the production of the present factories and to construct new ones in suitable locations. He received permission to build fortifications for protection against the local Bashkir tribes, and to search for iron and silver ores south of Ekaterinburg. The Instruction specifically gave Tatishchev authority to inspect the privately owned factories in the region and to enforce quality standards. He had the power to compel the privately owned factories to turn over to the State one-tenth of their iron supply. He could check the passports of all serf workers to see that the factory owners had acquired them

49

legally. It was estimated that less than 11 per cent of the serfs employed in the Demidov factories had proper papers. Last, but not least, Tatishchev had to conduct a geographical survey of the area and report any new finds of ores and precious stones to St. Petersburg. In a word, the Instruction gave Tatishchev the authority of a governor on all matters concerning the Urals metal industry. He could make all necessary administrative changes and enforce new regulations without first consulting the Commerce College in St. Petersburg.

Soon after he arrived in Ekaterinburg, Tatishchev began an inspection tour.[4] He checked the administrative records and found them in complete disorder.[5] Before he made any changes or enforced new regulations, he summoned all the factory owners and managers to a meeting in Ekaterinburg on 12 December to announce his plans and to ask for their cooperation.

Tatishchev opened the conference by presenting a short history of the Urals metal industry.[6] He explained that Peter the Great had encouraged its growth to provide Russia with high quality metal products in time of war. The industry had a great potential, and there were vast resources in the Urals region to ensure continued growth. Nevertheless, poor administration in the State plants and unfair competition among the entrepreneurs prevented efficient production. Tatishchev, therefore, announced that he was drawing up a "Factory Statute" to reform the State administration and a "Mining Statute" to prevent unfair practices among the entrepreneurs. He also demanded that the owners should follow the example of management in Sweden and Saxony and keep production and inventory records which would be made available to State inspectors. For both the "glory of the Fatherland" and production efficiency, he planned to translate the German metallurgical terminology into Russian. Many workers, of course, were unfamiliar with the German technical terms. Tatishchev then appointed A. I. Khrushchev in charge of the administrative records and of constructing lodgings and medical facilities for the workers. He closed the conference by asking for the cooperation of the factory owners and managers and by suggesting that more meetings be held in the future.

The Factory Statute which Tatishchev referred to during the meeting formed the foundation of his administration.[7] It established a collegial Secretariat in Ekaterinburg which controlled all judicial, technical, and social aspects of the privately owned factories, as well as the administration of the State system. Tatishchev gave particular attention to the Secretariat's judicial function. He outlined its duties and limitations, and delineated specific procedures for litigation of cases involving military

50

personnel, merchants, and foreign craftsmen. Moreover, the Secretariat had the power to levy fines and punishments on the factory owners for violations of its regulations. The Statute entrusted its treasury with the responsibility for keeping statistics on production from all the factories and for collecting taxes from the private sector.

The Statute also empowered the Secretariat to improve living conditions in the Urals community. For example, the treasury had to see that there were sufficient lodgings for serfs as well as wage laborers and merchants in the area. Tatishchev also held the Secretariat responsible for seeing that all workers received proper medical care and that the managers granted them certain holidays and Sundays free from work. According to Tatishchev's scheme, surveyors not only located new factory sites; he wanted them to serve as instructors in his proposed school system.

Early in 1735, Tatishchev established an inspection system and specified the factory managers' obligations. In an "Instruction to the Inspectors," Tatishchev authorized State officials to examine the plants, production records, and working conditions in all the Urals factories.[8] They had the responsibility of checking the finished products and marking them according to specifications made by the Admiralty College. They were also to enforce the regulations imposed by the Secretariat. The inspectors, however, were more than production "policemen." Tatishchev ordered them to assist factory managers in keeping accounts, and to make suggestions for increasing efficiency wherever possible. In fact, they had to keep factories functioning in the absence of the managers or owners, and intervene in disputes between managers and workers. They also suggested locations for new factory sites, based upon information from the Secretariat.

Tatishchev used the Instruction to improve the social and working conditions in the Urals factory complex. He compelled factory managers to compensate workers when ill, and he specifically forbade them to hold workers responsible for production losses which were not their fault. Factory owners now had to provide training facilities for craftsmen. He also required them to build and maintain elementary schools to teach all children in the area basic skills in reading, writing, and arithmetic. Taking into account religious needs, he directed the owners to build churches within walking distance of the workers' lodgings. Moreover, each factory had to construct a tavern where the workers could purchase liquor and supplies, and gather for recreation. Tatishchev, however, restricted the hours of sale of intoxicants to prevent absence from work due to drunkenness.

Tatishchev's inspectors began their duties by the end of 1735.[9] Although

51

he planned for 25 inspectors, he found only 13 craftsmen qualified for the assignment. He hoped that the Urals factory school system which he mentioned in the Instruction would provide the administration with a full complement of instructors within a few years. The inspectors were salaried officials, and they had to present formal reports to the Secretariat three times a year, as well as inform it of any violations of the factory regulations when they occurred.

Tatishchev's concern for social and working conditions did not end with the Instruction to the Inspectors. In 1736, he initiated a policy of granting religious toleration and permitting the Old Believers to work in the factories, and he personally drew up a curriculum for the factory schools.[10] The Old Believers were a religious sect which refused to recognize changes introduced into the Orthodox Church in the seventeenth century. Many fled to the Urals to escape persecution. In 1735, the Cabinet of her Imerpial Majesty ordered Tatishchev to take a census of the Old Believers in the area and commanded him to stamp out the heresy. They instructed him to exile the Old Believer clergy to Orthodox monasteries, and to force the peasants to work in the factories. Tatishchev, however, ignored the latter part of the order. Many of the Old Believers were already willingly working in the factories; and he knew that, if he tried to enforce the decree, many would flee and production would decrease. Moreover, the Old Believers were a serious people, and they refused to drink intoxicants. They were excellent workers, and there was a shortage of craftsmen in the Urals factories. Although he did take a census of their population, Tatishchev permitted them to live peacefully in the region, and even granted them freedom from reciting Orthodox prayers and catechetical lessons in the newly proposed school system.

In November 1736, Tatishchev issued an "Instruction Concerning the Order of Teaching in Schools Attached to the Urals Factories.[11] During his first administration in the Urals, he opened some schools chiefly to teach the sons of craftsmen and administrators. With the 1736 Instruction, he began a program to provide basic education for the children of all the inhabitants who lived near the factories. Although never completely implemented, the Instruction is extremely significant in the history of Russian education: at the time of its writing, Russia had no provisions or plans for mass education, and the clergy controlled all elementary schools.[12] Tatishchev's schools were controlled by the State, and they employed lay instructors.

In the Russian educational tradition, Tatishchev required that his teachers serve as models for their pupils. He specifically prohibited anyone who was considered a drunkard or thief from obtaining a position. The teachers should interest themselves in the pupils' home life and instill the fear of God into those in their charge. Tatishchev, however, departed from the traditional scheme by permitting, and actually preferring, lay people to qualify as instructors. Moreover, he emphasized that the teachers must have proper training in non-religious subjects, and that they must develop pedagogical skills.

The teacher had to arrive at the school before his pupils to see that the classroom was heated and prepared for the day's lessons. He had to keep attendance records, and if a pupil was absent due to illness, the teacher had to see that the child had medical attention. The teacher could hit the pupil on the hands and back (lightly), but Tatishchev forbade him to touch heads or faces.

School was in session six days a week and lasted throughout the year, with brief vacations in spring and fall. Tatishchev required all children in the area from 6 to 12 years of age to attend. His goal was to provide all with a basic education, and some with the proper foundation to qualify for further schooling. He suggested that pupils first learn to read and write and then study arithmetic, geometry, and architecture. Since the schools were attached to the factories, Tatishchev also wanted the pupils' education to be useful for their future tasks. The teachers also gave lessons in factory construction, mechanics, production techniques, and business methods. Children of the clergy studied music in place of the technical lessons. Although readings from Scripture and the catechism were part of the curriculum, Tatishchev placed greater emphasis on the secular subjects.

Within a year's time, Tatishchev established 12 elementary schools in the area.[13] More advanced pupils were sent to the Ekaterinburg School to receive further instruction in accounting, draftsmanship, and other subjects related to the metal industry. These students would qualify for positions as master craftsmen, factory managers, and inspectors. There were also German and Latin schools in Ekaterinburg for children of foreign craftsmen and the clergy. It is interesting to note that Tatishchev made his personal library of over a thousand volumes available to the students of the Ekaterinburg schools.

No doubt, Tatishchev had a great interest in his administrative reforms and in the newly established school system. However, it seems that acquiring more information about the Urals region was closer to his heart. Soon after his arrival in Ekaterinburg, Tatishchev dispatched a 92-item questionnaire to administrators in Siberia.[14] The first part of the questionnaire dealt with topography, the history of land features and settlements, climatic conditions, and the types of diseases which afflicted the population. He devoted the second part to questions concerning the various peoples of the region, their religions, social customs, and languages.

Shortly thereafter, he wrote a "Geographical Description of All Siberia," based upon information acquired from the questionnaire.[15] The first 12 chapters dealt with topography and mineral sources of the region. He also tried to establish Siberia's boundaries. He defined Siberia as the land mass bordered on the west by the Ural Mountains and extending eastward to the Gulf of Anadyr'. The Amur River formed the border with China on the south. The Vaygach Peninsula was Siberia's northernmost point. He then attempted to list as many rivers as possible; and noted their sources, lengths, and directions of flow. He speculated that rich deposits of iron and lead ores existed east of the Urals. Unfortunately, he completed only two articles on ethnography; at that point, he abandoned this project to work on a more extensive geographical survey.

In December 1736, Tatishchev sent an outline of the Geographical Description to the Cabinet of her Imperial Majesty; and, in early 1737, to the Academy of Sciences.[16] The Cabinet approved the project and sent a special order to the Governor of Siberia, A. B. Buturlin, commanding him to assist Tatishchev in gathering geographical information. Tatishchev then prepared an expanded questionnaire, "Proposition Concerning the Compilation of Russian History and Geography."[17]

Tatishchev divided the Proposition into three sections: the first contained 107 questions on topography and ethnography; the second, a group of 55 questions on the political, social, and religious customs of the peoples; and the third, a group of 17 questions dealing with the Mohammedans living in the region. In the last question, Tatishchev instructed his informants to compile dictionaries of the various languages whenever possible. He used the information gathered by the Proposition for his *Russian Geographical Lexicon* which he wrote at a later date.[18]

The two questionnaires also supplied Tatishchev with much information for his historical research. In spite of his administrative tasks, he managed to continue his historical studies. He carried on an active correspondence with Archbishop Theofan Prokopovich, with the historian Gottfried Bayer, and with other members of the Academy of Sciences.[19] In a letter of 15 August 1735 to Johann Schumacher, Tatishchev wrote that he was doing "not little work" in Russian and Finnish history.[20]

Indeed, Tatishchev's administrative reforms and production regulations imposed new requirements on the privately owned factories. The entrepreneurial families of Demidov, Stroganov, and Osokin had managed their factories for years without Government interference. Even though Tatishchev had their interests in mind when he drew up the various statutes and established a school system, they banded together to remove the factories from State control and ultimately to eliminate Tatishchev from the Ekaterinburg Secretariat.

On 11 March 1735, the managers of the Demidov, Stroganov, and Osokin factories petitioned Empress Anne to rescind Tatishchev's regulations.[21] They argued that it was impossible to keep an inventory of the supplies and to enforce strict quality control of the finished products. They estimated that it would take 10 men or more just to keep inventory. Moreover, they claimed that they could not afford to compensate workers when ill, grant holidays, and build schools and churches. At the close of their petition, the managers wrote that they regarded the new requirements as "insanity" on Tatishchev's part.

In May, both the Ekaterinburg Secretariat and the Commerce College replied to the managers' petition. The Secretariat, headed by Tatishchev, considered their arguments groundless.[22] Tatishchev explained that Swedish and Saxon factories kept production records, and Russian factories should do likewise. Moreover, he estimated that two—at most four—men could do the task adequately. As for refusing to pay craftsmen when ill, Tatishchev argued that the owners should do so out of Christian charity.

Tatishchev, however, devoted the larger portion of his reply to defending the factory schools. He explained that training in arithmetic, geometry, and grammar would create a more efficient work force. Moreover, children under 12 years of age could not work in the factories anyway, and education for everyone was necessary to rid the country of ignorance and superstition.

The Commerce College's reply, written by Baron P. P. Shafirov, wholeheartedly supported Tatishchev's regulations.[23] Shafirov wrote that the factory managers' complaints against inventory were invalid: factories in Sweden and Saxony kept accounts, and good bookkeeping procedures discouraged embezzlement and helped rationalize production. Moreover, the College recommended that the managers themselves carry out daily inspection tours and follow all suggestions made by the State inspectors.

The Commerce College also recognized the need for constructing schools for the workers' children. Although they recommended that only one school and church need be built for factories within walking distance, the College pointed out that education was entirely useful for the training of future workers. They also ordered the managers to compensate workers absent due to illness. In a word, the Commerce College directed the factory owners to comply with all of Tatishchev's regulations.

Soon after receiving the replies, the factory owners sought another means of freeing themselves from the Ekaterinburg Sceretariat. A. N. Demidov and Johann Biron, the Empress' Consort, schemed to remove Tatishchev from Ekaterinburg and to use the State factory system for their own profit.[24] Biron first removed the Urals factory system from the authority of the Commerce College and formed a separate Mining Directorate, which he directly controlled. He then replaced Shafirov with one of his own collaborators, Kurt von Schönberg. In the meantime, Demidov trumped up charges that Tatishchev confiscated his supplies, used his peasants to construct roads, and had threatened one of his factory managers with a whip. In April 1736, the Ekaterinburg Secretariat was stripped of its independent authority, and the privately owned factories were freed from its jurisdiction. A year later, Tatishchev was permanently removed from the Secretariat.

Although Tatishchev headed the Ekaterinburg Secretariat for only three years, his administration was extremely important for the growth of the Urals metal industry. During that time, he constructed 10 new State factories and planned 36 more.[25] If his proposed school system was not totally implemented, still the factory owners used it to train sons of the master craftsmen and administrators.[26]

All of Tatishchev's reforms and instructions demonstrated that he renewed the spirit of the Petrine era in the Urals. He obtained almost unlimited authority from the Commerce College to enable him to carry out reforms in spite of the political climate in St. Petersburg. Much in the Petrine tradition, he established a collegial Secretariat and tried to rationalize production by enforcing techniques and practices used in western Europe. The inspectors, too, served as a means to bring all the factories into daily contact with the central administration. Tatishchev did not set out to antagonize the entrepreneurs with his new regulations; he wanted to ensure that their products met the needs and standards of the Russian Government. In fact, inventory, bookkeeping, and quality control are basic practices in modern manufacturing.

Tatishchev's concern for the social needs and working conditions of the Urals workers was unique for his time. There was a constant labor shortage in the Urals factories, and he thought that he could attract craftsmen by providing them with good working conditions. He granted toleration to the Old Believers. His administration inspected the workers' lodgings, provided medical care, and compelled the factory managers to grant holidays and compensate workers when ill. Tatishchev's school system, though never completely implemented, would have been the most enlightened in Russia. He broke with tradition and emphasized secular subjects in the schools, and preferred lay instructors to clergy. Moreover, he planned to educate all children near the factories; and, in doing so, made his project the first attempt at mass education in Russia. Last, but not least, the State controlled the curriculum; up to that time, the clergy had a monopoly on elementary education in Russian schools. One can only speculate on the results if Tatishchev had remained in Ekaterinburg with unlimited authority for at least a decade!

In a word, during his three years in Ekaterinburg, Tatishchev tried to create an administration and society—an "empire," so to speak—which reflected in microcosm the spirit and goals of the Petrine era.

Chapter VIII

The Orenburg Commission

On 10 May 1737, V. N. Tatishchev was promoted to the rank of Privy Councilor and commissioned to take charge of the Orenburg Expedition which was making a geographical survey of the South Urals region. The Expedition was formed in 1734 by the geographer I. K. Kirilov to estabilsh fortresses and cities in that area and to seek trade routes to China and India. The Expedition was plagued with difficulties right from the start; and, in April 1737, Kirilov, its organizer and leader, died. Tatishchev did not exactly welcome the new assignment. He had been in ill health, and he was aware of the difficulties which he had to face. Although he headed the Expedition for only two years, he reformed and strengthened its administration and contributed significantly to the bringing of the South Urals region under Russian rule.

Little was known of the South Urals area until the Expedition began its work. A fortress had been built in the sixteenth century at the juncture of the Belaia and Ufa Rivers; nevertheless, there was little contact with the Bashkirs, Ural Cossacks, Kalmyks, Kirgiz, and Kazakhs which inhabited the area.[1] In the first half of the seventeenth century, Russian authorities imposed a small tax (iassak) in animal pelts on the Bashkirs and recognized their tribal government. From the mid-seventeenth century onward, however, the Bashkirs began a series of revolts to prevent the further extension of Russian authority. In the first decade of the eighteenth century, Russia used the military to try to quell the revolts. Later, Emperor Peter the Great recommended conciliation, and a precarious peace was maintained. In July 1728 the College of Foreign Affairs issued a charter which granted the Bashkirs a large degree of autonomy in tribal affairs. New revolts, however, broke out when Kirilov's Expedition entered the region.

In spring 1734, State Councilor I. K. Kirilov presented to the Senate a plan for the exploration of the South Urals region and for the subjugation of the inhabitants to Russian rule.[2] This project included the building of fortresses along the Samara and Ural (Iaik) Rivers and of a city, to be called Orenburg, where the Or joins the Ural River. He also planned to conduct a geographical survey of the region and to seek trade routes to China and India. Kirilov estimated that he would need approximately 100 men for the Expedition. He wanted to include natural scientists as well as architects and military personnel, to give the Expedition a research character.

Within a month's time, on 3 June 1734, Kirilov presented to the Senate a list of 75 individuals who wanted to join the Expedition. He recruited the remainder in Moscow. The Expedition included 12 geographers and several foreigners. John Castle, an English artist, painted the flora of the region; and John Elton, another Englishman, helped in the exploration. Johann Heinzelmann served as medical doctor and botanist for the Expedition. The future geographer of the Orenburg region, P. I. Rychkov, was then bookkeeper. After final preparations in Moscow, the Expedition left for Kazan', where a small military escort joined them. Kirilov ignored suggestions that he take along a large military detachment.

The Expedition entered the region in the spring of 1735. Kirilov and Colonel Alexis Tevkelev, who was of Tatar origin, planned the construction of Orenburg. Kirilov thought that its location at the juncture of the Or and Ural Rivers was an ideal position for trade with China and India. However, he did not take into consideration that it was particularly vulnerable to Bashkir attacks.

That fall, the Bashkirs launched full-scale revolts against the Expedition. Earlier, Tatishchev had tried to warn Kirilov of the impending attacks, but Kirilov did not recognize the danger. In fact, when the Expedition began its work, he divided his military force into two detachments and sent the weaker into the more troublesome area.[3] In November 1735, Kirilov held a conference at Menzelinsk to discuss a military campaign against the Bashkirs with General Rumiantsev. They decided that they should take firm measures against the Bashkir tribes. Since not all the Bashkirs were in revolt, they proposed to grant land and other privileges to those leaders or "elders" who remained loyal to Russian authority. Although Kirilov did not agree, Rumiantsev recommended, upon Tatishchev's suggestion, that, once the revolts were suppressed, Bashkir volunteers should be considered for Russian service in the war against Turkey.[4] By 1737, much of the area was under Russian control to the extent that local officials levied taxes in horses on the natives. Kirilov continued to consult with Tatishchev on all administrative matters.[5]

In 1736, Kirilov returned to St. Petersburg to report on the Expedition and to bring maps of the Ural River to the Academy of Sciences. He reported that his geographers were preparing a map of the entire Ufa area. Shortly after he returned to the Expedition, he died of consumption in April 1737.

Tatishchev was well acquainted with the Expedition's activities before he succeeded Kirilov. He had assisted Rumiansev in putting down Bashkir revolts, and he had maintained close contact with Kirilov. Moreover, the Menzelinsk conference adopted his idea to use the Bashkirs in Russian service. Although he did not exactly welcome his new assignment, the Expedition offered him greater opportunities to explore the South Urals region and to increase his geographical knowledge of the Russian Empire. In fact, earlier, he had been interested in opening the area to the metal industry. Perhaps most important, as the new leader of the Expedition, he worked to bring the South Urals region under Russian authority and to transform it administratively into an integral part of the Empire.

Before taking charge of the Expedition, Tatishchev inspected its records and studied its administration. He then wrote to the Vice Governor of Ufa, Shemiakin; to General Soimonov, who in the meantime had replaced Rumiantsev; and to Baron Ostermann and I. A. Cherkasskii in St. Petersburg for information and advice concerning his new task.[6] He reported to Ostermann and Cherkasskii that he found the Expedition's administration in great disorder.[7] In fact, he maintained that this disorder was one of the causes of the Bashkir revolts. Although the Bashkirs had made numerous complaints to local officials, nothing had been done to ameliorate conditions. Tatishchev held General Soimonov personally responsible for some of these problems. The General claimed ignorance of the situation, and he himself had been guilty of handing over Bashkir rebels to loyal tribesmen for cruel punishments. Moreover, Tatishchev thought that Soimonov was not capable of directing military affairs in the region. Tatishchev also accused one Lieutenant Bordukevich of collecting horses from the Bashkirs for his own use, under pretext of a Government tax. In general, Tatishchev felt that an orderly administration was entirely necessary for maintaining peace and extending Russian authority in Bashkir territory. Tatishchev officially took charge of the Expedition in late July 1737. His instructions from St. Petersburg simply ordered him to act with discretion.

Tatishchev's first official act was to call a conference at Menzelinsk with the chief military and administrative personnel of the Expedition.[8] At the close of the conference, it was decided to transfer the site of Orenburg to a more suitable and defensible location. In order to strengthen the Russian administration in Bashkiria, the conferees decided to create the Iset Province out of the Okunevsk, Shadrinsk, and Iset districts, with Fort Chebarkulsk as its center. Once they had determined Orenburg's new location, they proposed that it become the center for Bashkir affairs, and they also transferred the capital of Perm Province from Solikamsk to

Kungur, because of the latter's more central location. Tatishchev agreed to continue Kirilov's project of taking a census of the Bashkir population, but he also recommended that the mineral wealth of the area should be recorded. The Orenburg Expedition was thenceforth known as the Orenburg Commission.

Following the conference, Tatishchev discussed other matters in secret with General Soimonov, Colonel Tevkelev, and Vice Governor Shemiakin.[9] In a letter he wrote to Soimonov, Tatishchev noted that he considered the success of the Orenburg Commission absolutely essential for expanding Russian administration into the region and for assuring continued growth of the Empire. Since he believed that administrative corruption encouraged rebellions, Tatishchev decreed that the poll tax which was then under consideration for Bashkiria should not be levied until the bureaucracy was improved. In fact, Tatishchev suspended the collection of fees in horses from the Bashkirs until more forts could be built. He then announced that he planned to move Orenburg to Krasnaia Gora, approximately 130 miles west of Kirilov's original location.[10]

There was little difficulty in transferring Orenburg to its new site. Construction at Kirilov's location had progressed very slowly; by summer 1737 only the foundations had been made. In fact, the slow pace led Tatishchev to suspect that Kirilov's architects were embezzling construction funds. Tatishchev, however, did not abandon the original location of Orenburg. The site was renamed Orsk, and Tatishchev sent Ivan Rychkov, father of P. I. Rychkov, there to improve conditions and to establish a marketing center.

Unfortunately, Tatishchev's administrative work in the Orenburg Commission was interrupted by a new series of Bashkir revolts. In early 1737, before Tatishchev took charge, the Bashkirs began to complain about taxes and administrative corruption.[11] The natives had legitimate grievances. It had become common practice for the Russian tax collectors to charge the Bashkirs more than their just fees, and to pocket the surplus. There was also widespread famine in Bashkiria at that time. Kirilov and Soimonov had confiscated Bashkir supplies whenever possible to prevent future revolts. This policy, however, led only to more rebellions, since the tribesmen would attack settlements to acquire food. Although the Bashkirs had valid complaints against the Russians, the real cause for the new series of revolts was that they wanted to prevent the Empire from extending its authority into their region.

During the spring of 1737, Bashkirs who were loyal to the Empire reported to Russian officials that there would be a new series of revolts. Shortly after taking charge of the Orenburg Commission, Tatishchev sent ammunition and some troops to aid the loyal Bashkirs in the event of rebellion. Tatishchev did not have long to wait. In early August, several tribes revolted; and, by late fall, several villages of the loyal Bashkirs had been destroyed.

Tatishchev handled the revolts quite differently than did Kirilov in 1735. For one thing, Tatishchev did not plan a large-scale military campaign against the Bashkirs. Instead, he promised to deal mercifully with any tribesman who surrendered to the Empire, and he used the military only in retaliation and as a threat. He decreed that those who voluntarily took an oath of loyalty to the Empress would be fined one horse, and even the fine would be suspended if the warrior brought a rebellious elder with him to one of the Russian forts. When this policy proved only partially successful, Tatishchev called another conference at Menzelinsk in December 1737.

Although Tatishchev called the second conference at Menzelinsk to deal with the immediate problem of the Bashkir revolts, some of the measures adopted that December became the basis of his and succeeding administrations of the Orenburg Commission. First of all, Tatishchev promised the Bashkirs that he would do everything possible to correct administrative abuses.[12] He placed loyal Bashkir elders, rather than Russian officials, in charge of collecting taxes for the Empire. In that way, he eliminated one of the major complaints. He further demonstrated his understanding of the difficult situation the Bashkirs faced after Kirilov's military campaigns by suspending the collection of taxes for a year's time. He was insistent, however, that each tribesman who participated in the revolt turn over one horse to the Empire. Last, but not least, he promised to establish a court system throughout Bashkiria and to make provisions for Russian administrators to keep records of Bashkir land transactions to prevent future quarrels among the tribesmen.

Although most of the Bashkir elders accepted Tatishchev's new resolutions, a few obstinate leaders continued the rebellion. The situation improved until late winter, when the Kazakhs broke their agreement with the Empire. When the Bashkir revolts resumed, Tatishchev called upon Kazakh Khan Abul Hair to assist the Russian troops in a limited campaign.[13] At first, the Kazakhs fought loyally beside the Russians. But, in late February 1738, one of the Bashkir leaders, Bepen Trupberdin, persuaded Abul Hair to join his rebellion against the extension of Russian authority into the region. Bepen thereupon had Abul Hair marry a Bashkir woman to ensure the Khan's loyalty to his cause.

When Tatishchev learned of Abul Hair's defection, he invited the Khan to meet with him for a conference at Orenburg (Orsk).[14] Abul

Hair camped near the city at the end of July; and, after some persuasion, he agreed to meet with Tatishchev. Tatishchev prepared an impressive ceremony—complete with full-dress uniforms, speeches, and cannonade—to greet the Khan. Following the introductory pomp, Tatishchev held a huge banquet in honor of the Khan. After the festivities, Tatishchev discussed with Abul Hair his disloyalty to the Empress of Russia. Abul Hair admitted that he had broken his oath to the Empress, and explained that he had joined the Bashkirs so that he would be remembered as a great warrior among his own people. Tatishchev then told the Khan of the many advantages the Kazakhs could gain by remaining loyal to the Empress. Abul Hair was particularly impressed when Tatishchev told him that, if he were loyal, all Europe would read about him and learn of his greatness. Tatishchev thereupon persuaded Abul Hair to reaffirm his oath; and, afterwards, the rebellion was limited to Bepen Trupberdin's followers.

Tatishchev's methods in dealing with Abul Hair, and with the Bashkirs in general, were sound ones. During the seventeenth century, Siberian administrators often quelled uprisings by inviting the tribal chieftains to impressive banquets.[15] In fact, local officials often left information for their successors on what type of ceremonies impressed the tribal chiefs. Having been an administrator in the Urals region for nearly two decades, Tatishchev obviously had become familiar with this practice. When Tatishchev reported his conversation with Abul Hair to the Empress, he wrote that the Bashkirs and other frontier people were fierce warriors, and that administrators had to use discretion in dealing with them. Moreover, he explained that he did not have sufficient funds to carry out a long military campaign.

During the remainder of 1738, the most obstinate Bashkir elders surrendered to Tatishchev and took a loyalty oath to the Empress.[16] Tatishchev ordered lenient treatment, even to those who surrendered at this late date. Only in one case did he demand extreme punishment. When Bepen Trupberdin was captured, Tatishchev ordered him broken upon the wheel as an example, to prevent future uprisings. In general, Tatishchev's pacification policy was so successful that, by the end of his administration, he was able to use a Bashkir military contingent for Russian service in the war against Turkey. Unfortunately, his broader plan for organizing the Bashkirs into detachments similar to the Cossacks was interrupted by his return to St. Petersburg.

Besides his military and administrative duties, Tatishchev also continued the geographical exploration begun by Kirilov.[17] In 1738, with the help of others, he completed maps of the Ural, Samara, and Volga Rivers.

Because of his geographical knowledge of the region, he was asked to find a suitable location for the tribe of Kalmyk Princess Anna Taishina, who had converted to Orthodoxy.[18] To follow through with Kirilov's plans to find new trade routes with the East, he dispatched a caravan to Samarkand to establish commercial ties with Bukhara.[19]

In the summer of 1738, Tatishchev requested permission to return to St. Petersburg to report on the Orenburg Commission and to explain his Bashkir policy to the Empress.[20] In the meantime, however, Colonel Tevkelev and others had complained that Tatishchev had embezzled State funds and was responsible for the Commission's administrative disorder. After delegating his authority to Prince Vasilii Urusov, Tatishchev left Orenburg at the end of 1738. He was relieved of his duties with the Orenburg Commission shortly thereafter.

Although Tatishchev headed the Orenburg Commission for less than two years, his administration was a pivotal one in the history of Russia's expansion into the Urals region. Much more than Kirilov, Tatishchev is to be credited with extending Russian authority into the area. True, Kirilov formed the Expedition and led it into the South Urals. Nevertheless, Kirilov was more concerned with finding trade routes and exploring the area than with establishing Russian authority there. Tatishchev, however, placed greater emphasis on an efficient administration and on bringing the area into the Empire. In a word, Kirilov formed the Orenburg *Expedition,* and Tatishchev headed the Orenburg *Commission.*

Tatishchev's reforming of Kirilov's Expedition administration is of particular interest. To be sure, it sounded good for Tatishchev to report to St. Petersburg that Kirilov's administration was in disorder, and then proceed to reform it. Nevertheless, Tatishchev tried to implant the values and characteristics of the Petrine bureaucracy wherever he was in charge. When he took over the Expedition, he noticed that there was no real administrative system. Moreover, several military officers were not suited for their tasks. A reform of the administration was absolutely necessary before he could make the Empire's influence felt in the region.

Tatishchev's ultimate goal was to bring the frontier region under the authority of the central administration in St. Petersburg. Similar to his objectives when in charge of the Urals metal industry, Tatishchev wanted to incorporate the area into the Empire and to transplant there the laws, customs, and civilization of European Russia. Prior to his administration, Russian authorities did not have a consistent policy towards the South Urals area and its inhabitants. Tatishchev took the first important step in extending Russian authority into the region. As the historian

Boris Nolde has observed, Tatishchev's having formed a Bashkir contingent for Russian service ". . . marked a new stage in the Russian acquisition, and it determined all subsequent policies in Bashkiria."[21] Indeed, Tatishchev achieved his success through discretion, good management, and diplomacy—marks of a true statesman.

No one in Russia was better suited for this task. Tatishchev had both the necessary experience and a personal commitment to bring Bashkiria under the authority of the Empire. During his administration of the Urals factory system, he had come into contact with the inhabitants of the South Urals region, and he was aware of the problems of Russia's eastward expansion. He had kept abreast of Kirilov's work, and had made suggestions for dealing with the natives. Moreover, Tatishchev was an experienced and successful administrator; on previous occasions, he had thrived on reforming and increasing the efficiency of Government authority, and he came to identify himself with these accomplishments. Tatishchev early understood the problems and necessity of integrating the newly acquired areas into the Empire. From his dealings with the Bashkirs and other tribes, he realized the importance of Russia's adopting a clear and practical policy towards its frontier regions. As demonstrated in his negotiations with Abul Hair, he wanted to "sell" the Empire to the Bashkirs by explaining the advantages of Russian rule, and the only way that he could give the local tribes a sense of belonging to the Russian (multi-national) State was by impressing upon them the unifying symbol of the monarchy.

Perhaps his very appointment to succeed Kirilov stands as convincing evidence that Tatishchev was the most suitable person for the assignment. If Biron and others in St. Petersburg opposed his policies in the Urals factory administration, they in no way prevented him from taking charge of the Orenburg Expedition. Whom else could they have appointed? Tatishchev was arleady in the Urals; and, as leader of the Orenburg Expedition, he no longer interfered in Biron's schemes in the metal industry. And by the time he was recalled to St. Petersburg, Tatishchev had already accomplished the most important part of his misson.

Within two years, V. N. Tatishchev brought Russian authority to the South Urals and established definite policies in the Empire's dealings with the Bashkirs. His successors merely continued those policies for the remainder of the century.

Chapter IX

Imprisonment

For the next year and a half, from February 1739 until August 1741, V. N. Tatishchev remained in St. Petersburg. During that time, he submitted a project to the Senate for a geographical survey of Russia and wrote his own plan for a regional reform of the Empire. The period also proved to be the most trying in his career as a civil servant. He had to answer to embezzlement charges on two occasions, and he was imprisoned for several months during the second investigation. Nevertheless, during his imprisonment or shortly thereafter, he wrote a *Testament*[1] in which he attempted to outline the duties and responsibilities of the Russian gentry.

Shortly after his return from the Orenburg region, Tatishchev presented an account of the Commission's progress to the Cabinet of her Imperial Majesty and delivered maps and geographical information to the Academy of Sciences.[2] These materials included maps of the Moscow, Volga, and Chussavaia Rivers. He also was able to explain satisfactorily to the Cabinet about embezzlement charges made against him during his leadership of the Commission. On 10 April 1739, he received a request from the Senate to report on the progress of work on the geography of the Orenburg region.

When Tatishchev made his presentation on the 30th of April, he concentrated on impressing upon the Senate the necessity of compiling a geography and atlas of the entire Russian Empire, as well as reporting on the progress of the Orenburg Commission.[3] Tatishchev understood quite well what such a project involved, for his interest in geography dated back to 1719, when he presented to Peter the Great a plan for a land survey of the Empire. Moreover, during his second administration of the Urals factory system, he conducted his own geographical survey of Siberia and gathered data for his *Geographical Lexicon*.[4]

Tatishchev began his presentation by reporting that he had already given the Commission's geographical material to the members of the Academy, and that he had discussed the data with the professors. He added, however, that one of the members, Professor Delisle, had dealt him a "rebuff," and that he therefore feared that the cartographical project was not progressing rapidly enough. For one thing, Delisle, according to Tatishchev, was not making complete use of Kirilov's materials and was procrastinating by claiming that he did not have a sufficient quantity of accurate maps. Tatishchev suggested that Delisle should use all the materials he had at hand until more maps and surveys could be compiled.

Immediately following the report, Tatishchev commented on the uses and necessity of a complete geographical description and atlas of the Empire. He pointed out that all of Russia's geographical works were then written in foreign languages. Moreover, the best of these, Johannes Gibner's *Kurze Fragen aus der neun und alten Geographie*, did not contain adequate historical background information. He argued that a complete geographical survey was absolutely necessary to the gentry, to military and civil officials, and to students. In fact, all Europe would benefit from a Russian atlas and complete land survey. Moreover, this project was absolutely necessary before the Senate could consider the regional reorganization of the Empire.

Tatishchev then turned to his own geographical projects. He explained that, when he was in charge of the Urals factory system, he attempted to compile his own geographical survey of Siberia, and that he hoped to complete this work in the future. He admitted, however, that he lacked the knowledge of physics and astronomy, as well as of the history of Russia, which he considered necessary to prepare a geography of the entire Empire. This task was beyond the ability of one individual. He therefore suggested that such a project be placed under the supervision of the Academy, and that the State assume the expense of importing personnel and equipment from England and France.

Tatishchev's method of gathering information for an atlas and geographical survey of the Empire was quite elaborate for his time. He suggested that teams of surveyors proceed eastward from the Polish border. They were to survey the entire Empire and keep meticulous accounts of their progress. Moreover, they should keep reports of all mineral finds and make these records available to local officials. Throughout the survey, these groups would maintain close contact with each other and furnish Professor Delisle with all of their information. He also proposed that permanent observatories should be constructed in various locations.

Besides his plans for the survey proper, Tatishchev recommended to the Senate that they commission 10 or 15 men from the Academy to translate the more important foreign geography works into the Russian language. Accordingly, he proposed that native Russians be trained in geography to assist the foreign personnel assigned to the survey. In that way, Russians would learn the most modern survey techniques, and eliminate the necessity of importing personnel for future exploration. He then added that the *Geographical Lexicon* which he was compiling would also help in increasing the geographical knowledge of the Empire. Tatishchev estimated that it would take approximately three years to complete his survey plan.

Although the Senate did not adopt his elaborate land survey plans, Tatishchev was successful in reviving interest in the project. Shortly thereafter, a special department was created in the Academy to compile materials for an atlas of the Russian Empire.[5] In 1745, the Academy published a *Russian Atlas* which consisted of one map of the entire Empire and 19 particular maps. The publication of the *Russian Atlas* owed a great deal to Tatishchev's intervention and insistence on the completion of the project.

Tatishchev, however, did not limit his activities to informing Delisle and reporting to the Senate. During 1739 and early 1740, he turned his attention to another geographical project in which he proposed a reorganization of the Empire in accord with his historical and geographical divisions. He thought that the eastward expansion necessitated a further rationalization of Peter the Great's initial administrative organization of the Empire. He entitled the work "Russia, or as it is Called Today, Rossiia."[6]

Tatishchev characteristically began his proposal by presenting a sketch of Russia's history. He divided the summary into five stages: first, ancient times until the calling of Riurik; second, from the founding of the monarchy in 862 to the Mongol invasion in the thirteenth century; third, the Tatar domination until Ivan III freed Russia from the Mongol yoke; fourth, the "Time of Troubles" to the election of Michael Romanov; and, last, the happy rule of the Romanovs. Tatishchev explained that the name of the country, "Russia," was derived from the Sarmatian word "Rus," which meant the colors black or red. The Sarmatians used "Rus" to describe the people who lived near Novgorod in early times.[7]

According to Tatishchev's account, the first division was in accord with the boundaries which separated the early peoples who inhabited the Russian land: first, the territory of the "Great Rus," who lived near Novgorod; and, second, the "Little Rus"—primarily the Drevliane tribe—who inhabited the area to the south; then, the "White Rus," who, Tatishchev wrote, were mainly Sarmatians prior to the calling of Riurik; fourth, the "Chervonaia Rus," whose name was derived from the town of Cherven in their region. He listed the "Chernaia Rus," and admitted that he lacked any knowledge of these people. He mentioned that the Bulgars inhabited the Volga region and noted that Tatars lived to the east. Tsar Ivan III accomplished the first administrative division of the Muscovite State. He created three areas: Vladimir, Novgorod, and Riazan; Ivan IV added Kazan'. Later, Tsar Alexis divided Russia into 12 regions, and Peter the Great created an Empire of eight gubernii.

After listing the more important topographical features of the Empire, i.e., seas, rivers, lakes, mountains, etc., Tatishchev presented his plan for its administrative territorial reorganization. His project called for six gubernii, which in turn would be divided into vice-gubernii, provinces, and city regions. He would have established a Velikorusskaia, or Great Russia, Guberniia in northwest Russia centering around St. Petersburg. Belorusskaia, or White Russia, followed, with Moscow for its administrative center.[8] Bolgarskaia Guberniia would have consisted of Kazan', Astrakhan, and the entire new Siberian territories governed from Kazan'. Malorusskaia, or Little Russia, followed, which included the entire area between the Polish and Turkish borders. Tatishchev placed the Don River region in its own Donakaia or Voronezhakaia Guberniia, with its capital at Voronezh. The Baltic area bordering Lithuania and Courland would have formed its own Rizhakaia Guberniia, with a capital at Revel. Following the proposed territorial reorganization, Tatishchev described the peoples, animals, vegetation, mineral wealth, and industry particular to each region, devoting a disproportionately greater length of the discussion to Siberia.

"Russia, or as it is Called Today, Rossiia" has a greater importance than just a plan for the administrative reorganization of the Empire. In his project, Tatishchev emphasized the historical significance of each of his divisions. He recognized that, even from the earliest times, many different peoples inhabited the Russian land; and he attempted to establish territorial boundaries within the context of the historical development of each of these various peoples. For example, Velikorusskaia Guberniia encompassed, more or less, the area once inhabited by the "Great Rus." Perhaps even more important, Tatishchev's project was an argument to incorporate the new Siberian territories into the Empire rather than to regard them as a mere frontier region, which explains why he devoted a lengthy discussion to the natural wealth of the area. Although Tatishchev's reorganization was never implemented, it is indeed worthy of study, and the Senate referred to it in 1743-1744 when territorial reform was again seriously considered. Since "Russia, or as it is Called Today, Rossiia" was considered at the time the best summary of Russian geography, it was translated into German as "Eine Kurze Geographie von Russland" for study by the foreign members of the Academy.

In the spring of 1740, however, Tatishchev's work in geography was interrupted. Although Tatishchev had explained his activities in the Orenburg Commission satisfactorily to the Cabinet of her Imperial Majesty, others wished to pursue the matter further. In a letter dated 11 March 1739 to Biron, Count Golovkin charged Tatishchev with having accepted bribes and having failed to report the exact location of Orenburg.[9] Golovkin assured Biron that Colonel Tevkelev, among others, would testify to Tatishchev's guilt.

In early 1740, Golovkin headed a commission to investigate the charges, and Tatishchev was imprisoned in the Peter-Paul Fortress for the duration of the trial.[10] By the end of that summer, however, all of the charges had been dropped, with the exception of the Inozemtsev case. According to this charge, in 1737 Tatishchev had angrily interrogated the wife of the merchant-official Semën Inozemtsev as to the whereabouts of her husband. When the wife refused to answer, Tatishchev threatened to place her under arrest. Another merchant, one Boris Pushnikov, testified that Tatishchev later had been willing to accept a bribe of 500 rubles not to imprison her. Pushnikov testified that Tatishchev and Inozemtsev had argued earlier, and that Tatishchev had a personal dislike for Inozemtsev. Tatishchev apparently had no explanation for this charge, and Golovkin's commission found him guilty of bribery. Tatishchev was subsequently removed from Government service and deprived of his rank of Privy Councilor.

At the same time that Golovkin's commission investigated the charges against Tatishchev, another commission was reviewing the case of Artemii Pertovich Volynskii and his "Confidants," charged with treason. Although Tatishchev was not tried along with Volynskii's Confidants, he probably was involved in their activities to some degree. In fact, Volynskii's biographer, D. M. Korsakov,[11] listed Tatishchev among the five most important Confidants, and Hans Rogger in his *National Consciousness in Eighteenth Century Russia* mentioned that Tatishchev was a member of the Volynskii circle in the early 1730's.[12] Although Conrad Grau disclaimed Tatishchev's participation in the circle, he noted that Tatishchev was in agreement with Volynskii's ideas.[13] Although it is impossible to determine exactly from the available material Tatishchev's relationship with the Volynskii circle, no biography of him would be complete without giving attention to this important episode.

Born in 1689, Volynskii entered State service in 1704 at the age of 16.[14] In 1711, he made the personal acquaintance of Peter the Great. In the 1720's, he served as Governor, first of Kazan' and later of Astrakhan. Following the succession crisis of 1730, Volynskii attached himself to the royal court and became a close friend of the Empress' consort, Biron. By early 1738, Biron appointed Volynskii as a permanent member of the Cabinet of her Imperial Majesty, and he also served as secretary of the War, Admiralty, and Foreign Affairs Colleges. In the following year, Biron entrusted Volynskii to report to the Empress on Cabinet business.

According to Korsakov, Volynskii schemed to secure a position near the Empress following the succession crisis of 1730, so that he could implement reforms and rid Russia of its foreign rulers such as Biron and Munnich. Although he was not in Moscow in 1730, he studied the various projects submitted to the Empress at that time; and, as early as 1731, he formed a circle of close friends to discuss ideas for reforms. The more prominent members of the circle in the early years were: General F. I. Soimonov, the court architect P. I. Eropkin, A. F. Khrushchev, Count Platon Musin-Pushkin, Princes A. D. Kantemir and G. A. Urusov, and V. N. Tatishchev.[15] Korsakov stated that Tatishchev read portions of his *Russian History* to the members of the group, who then would make comparisons between Russia during their time and during the "Time of Troubles."

In the mid-1730's, Volynskii began to draft reform projects based upon the discussions with members of his circle.[16] Although he attempted to burn these documents before his arrest in 1740, fragments of a "General Project" were not destroyed. On the basis of these fragments, it would seem that the main purpose of Volynskii's plans was to preserve the autocracy in Russia In fact, he greatly disapproved of the gentry's having tried to limit the power of the monarchy in 1730. Although he approved of assistance to the Empress by the Cabinet of her Imperial Majesty, he noted that at that time its members were more involved in personal rivalries than in governing the Empire. But, more important, Volynskii argued that only native Russians should serve in the Cabinet, since rule by foreigners ruined the country. The nobility, for their part, should serve as members of the Senate and in various civil offices; they should protect the monarchy rather than seek to limit its authority. According to the General Project, the Senate would be divided into two houses, with the Generality serving in the upper chamber and the gentry in the lower house.

Volynskii's General Project also included economic and educational reforms. He suggested that the State should take measures to increase trade and to protect merchants. To retain capital within the Empire, he wished to prohibit Russian merchants from joining foreign trading companies. Volynskii recognized that Russia needed well-trained people in the various professions. He therefore recommended that the State establish professional schools to train craftsmen and merchants, and academies to train the clergy; in fact, he held the clergy responsible for educating the peasantry, and advocated a general reform in the Orthodox Church.

Volynskii wrote a synopsis of his ideas in a letter which he presented to Empress Anne during the early spring of 1734. He subsequently began to draft his General Project upon her request. Eropkin and Khrushchev helped him prepare the draft, and Musin-Pushkin made suggestions for the parts dealing with economics. Volynskii said that he showed copies of the Project to both Ostermann and Tatishchev. Volynskii was arrested on 12 April 1739 before he had a chance to submit the General Project to the Empress. The other members of the circle were apprehended a few days later. Tatishchev, however, was already in prison awaiting the outcome of his own inquisition.

Biron immediately established a commission which charged Volynskii with having plotted to overthrow the monarchy and to declare himself ruler of Russia. Fragments of his General Project were introduced as evidence, and it seems that Biron had little or no difficulty in convincing the Empress of Volynskii's guilt. Volynskii, Eropkin, and Khrushchev were executed on 21 July 1740, and other members of the circle were either imprisoned or executed. Tatishchev escaped charges of having been implicated in the Volynskii affair.

Even though Tatishchev was not tried as a member of the Volynskii circle, this certainly does not exclude the possibility or the probability of his participation in the affair. For one thing, Tatishchev knew and worked closely with several members of the circle from time to time. He worked with Musin-Pushkin in the Currency Control and was, with Prince Kantemir, a member of the Learned Guard. He served in the Urals with Khrushchev and Soimonov. All were "reform-minded" individuals, and they most likely discussed the ideas contained in the General Project whenever they met. Moreover, Volynskii's General Project followed the same lines as Tatishchev's 1730 reform plan. And, finally, Volynskii himself said that Tatishchev had read his Project.

If Tatishchev were a member of the Volynskii plot, how did he escape investigation and punishment? There may be several answers this question. The proceedings against Volynskii may have been a very personal matter for Biron. Earlier, Biron had had complete confidence in Volynskii, and it is possible that he was angry at his Russian friend for having betrayed his trust. Also, Biron may have genuinely feared that Volynskii had planned a *coup d'état*. Biron, indeed, did not like Tatishchev. However, the Duke of Courland did not fear that Tatishchev would threaten his position. Perhaps even more important, Tatishchev was already in prison; and, considering his ill health and his geographical activities, there was little time for him to become active in the plot. Moreover, as Conrad Grau has suggested, Empress Anne may have excused Tatishchev from the Volynskii affair as a favor for his having helped to overthrow Golitsyn and the oligarchy in 1730.[17] Be this as it may, Tatishchev was spared the burden of another investigation, even though he was eventually discredited and deprived of rank by a different commission.

Sometime in 1740, probably during his own and Volynskii's trials, Tatishchev wrote a *Testament* in which he gave fatherly advice and willed all of his possessions to his son Evgraf.[18] More important, Tatishchev wrote the *Testament* to offer to the Russian nobility a program by which they could retain their identity and honor as a class, and at the same time fulfill the new obligations imposed upon them by the new Petrine service system. Tatishchev obviously reflected a great deal on this problem, and the recommendations which he made in 1740 were much more specific than those which he included in his "Conversation" of 1733.[19]

Similar to his recommendations in the "Conversation," Tatishchev suggested that the nobility obtain adequate training and education before entry into State service. All of the gentry should learn writing, arithmetic, geometry, and the military sciences; and those who planned to enter the civil service should study the German language, geography, and Russian history. They should also have a basic knowledge of civil and military law codes. The gentry were not to neglect their religious education. Tatishchev, therefore, recommended that they read the Bible and study the writings of the church fathers and the reformers of Western Europe.

According to Tatishchev's formula, the nobility could choose among three careers in State service: the military, civil service, and attendance at the imperial court. (Since the time of Peter the Great, the nobility had been discouraged from entering the clergy.) Nobles usually entered the military first. Tatishchev recommended that one serve in the military between his 18th and his 25th years. If entered too early, he wrote, military life could do physical harm or corrupt the morals of a young man. Also, an older person would be too independent and soft for the rigorous and disciplined life of a soldier. A soldier had to be courageous; but, he continued, foolhardy adventurers did just as much a disservice to the State as cowards.

Activities in civil administration, according to Tatishchev, were the highest form of service which the gentry could render to the Govern-

73

ment. It took more knowledge and skill to function as a civil official than in the military service. Moreover, without an orderly administration, nothing could be accomplished. Peter the Great had recognized the importance of having well-trained officials when he assigned young gentry-men to the various colleges to learn the art of good administration. However, Tatishchev lamented, this practice had been discontinued after the Emperor's death.

Tatishchev realized, consciously or unconsciously, that the civil service created by Peter the Great demanded a new sense of duty from the gentry. The gentry officials, indeed the entire nobility as a class, should guard State interests as if they were their own, and always protect the sovereignty and honor of the monarch. According to Tatishchev's analysis, the course of Russian history taught that the absolute authority of the monarchy must be preserved. From his own experience, Tatishchev suggested that a civil servant should never refuse anything to or ask for anything from his superiors. An official must be just, especially in the litigation of judicial procedures. Nevertheless, he should always guard the interests of the State in these matters—sometimes even at the expense of the individual involved.

If Tatishchev emphasized the importance of the civil service, he by no means belittled the contributions which nobles could make in attendance at the imperial court.[20] In fact, he pointed out that the word "noble" (dvorianin) was derived from the word for "court" (dvor). The nobles' presence enhanced the court, and those nearest the sovereign should be most helpful in advising him. Tatishchev observed, however, that, during the reign of Empress Anne, courtiers intrigued and sought gifts from the monarch in their own interests. According to Tatishchev, the nobles nearest the throne should refrain from intrigue, hypocrisy, and personal rewards; rather, they should take upon themselves the improvement of Russia's culture and of her image among other nations.

A noble's service continued into his retirement. Tatishchev suggested that an official request release from duty after reaching age 50. Then, the retired noble should devote his time to managing his estate efficiently. He should look after the spiritual needs and, more important, the education of his peasants. In a word, a nobleman's concern for those in his charge was fulfilling another of his obligations; he again would be rendering a "service" to the State.

There is every indication that Tatishchev wrote the *Testament* for a wider audience than his son. At the close, he cautioned his son that, if his writings fell into the hands of others, they might condemn his words. Similarly, he asked were not the words of Christ and the Apostles criticized and misused? Moreover, if Tatishchev were writing only for his son, he would not have had to be so explicit in outlining the three careers and would not have had to bother to explain the function of courtiers. Tatishchev's son, in fact, knew of his father's ideas concerning the Russian nobility and State service from the "Conversation" of 1733. Indeed, because of its relevance, the *Testament* was the first of his writings to be published.

When he wrote the *Testament*, Tatishchev no doubt thought that it would be his final act. He was ill, and imprisonment could only have aggravated his condition. Moreover, at that time he must have felt a constant threat of being dragged into the proceedings against Volynskii. It is no small surprise that he would again turn to the problem of the Russian nobility. Similar to the events during his stay in Moscow in 1731-1734, he was discredited, deprived of his rank, and dismissed from State service. He naturally reflected upon the situation which had brought about his disgrace. He saw better than any Russian of his time the turmoil among the nobility. He therefore proposed a possible solution to the problem in what he may have considered to be his final contribution to the Russian State and society.

Tatishchev tried to retain the nobility as an élite within the Petrine service system. According to his formula, the gentry could acquire its identity through education and through their new responsibilities in the civil service. Nor did Tatishchev forget the particular position which the upper nobility or Generality held in pre-Petrine Russia. He recognized their importance by suggesting that they serve as courtiers. They were to have the privilege of being in the monarch's presence. More important, however, Tatishchev gave them the responsbiility of advising the sovereign and of assuming the cultural leadership of Russia. In this way, the old noble families would gain distinction and have a function in performing a very necessary service to the State. They would no longer feel deprived of their identity and usefulness and, therefore, would seek to protect rather than limit the authority of the monarch.

Fortunately, the *Testament* was not Tatishchev's final contribution to the State. Before fall 1740, he was released from prison, though still deprived of his rank.[21] From that November until August of the following year, he helped with the cartographical work at the Academy and continued to work on his *Russian History*.

Within the century following Tatishchev's death, the nobility followed Tatishchev's formula to a significant degree. The gentry and members of the pre-Petrine upper nobility retained their social position and dignity by rendering service to the State. In fact, the nobility soon distinguished themselves by their absorption of European culture. Even though his *Testament* was published shortly after his death, that is not to say that Tatishchev alone was responsible for the transformation. Perhaps it is more accurate to say that he was the first to reflect upon the problems of the nobility as a class in the Russia of that time, and the first to offer a plausible solution for their quest for an identity.

Chapter X

Last Years in State Service

V. N. Tatishchev spent his last four years of State service in the frontier regions. On 31 July 1741, the College of Foreign Affairs ordered him to take charge of a newly formed Kalmyk Commission. The College established this Commission to restore peace and order among the Kalmyk tribes in the Volga River valley. Six months later, however, Tatishchev was appointed Governor of Astrakhan. During this period, Tatishchev continued to serve with the same fixed purposes he had when in charge of the Urals factory system and the Orenburg Commission. He increased the efficiency of civil administration and used his authority to give the State an active role in economic development in Astrakhan Guberniia.

Tatishchev's new position, and reinstatement in the rank of Privy Councilor, in no way freed him from charges of embezzlement.[1] In fact, Golovkin made certain that Tatishchev received only half salary on the Commission. The College's choice of Tatishchev to head the Commission was both an insult to the Privy Councilor and a practical decision. At that time, Tatishchev was 55 years old and in ill health. Rather than assigning him to more comfortable duties in St. Petersburg or Moscow, the College sent him to the frontier regions. Then again, Tatishchev was probably the best choice for the Commission. He was an experienced administrator, and he had established peace in the frontier among the Bashkirs when in charge of the Orenburg Commission. Moreover, during those years, he had assisted in Kalmyk affairs. Indeed, perhaps his reinstatement to service was due to his competence as an administrator and previous success in the frontier region. Before he left St. Petersburg, the College of Foreign Affairs granted him an allowance of 1,000 rubles for expenses, and placed him in "acting command" of all matters pertaining to the Kalmyks.

The difficulty of Tatishchev's task was due to the peculiar relationship maintained between the Russian Empire and the Kalmyks.[2] When this nomadic, Turcic-speaking, and Buddhist people migrated into the Volga region in the early seventeenth century, they sought Russian protection from the Tatars, Nogais, and Kirgiz who also inhabited the area. In turn, the Kalmyks accepted Russian authority, though they were permitted to retain their own tribal government and customs. Although minor insurrections broke out from time to time in the seventeenth century, there were no large-scale disturbances along the Volga. Russian-Kalmyk relations were particularly good during the reign of Peter the Great. In fact, Peter once visited their Khan Aiuka, an act which confirmed the cordial relations betwen the Empire and the Kalmyks. Affairs improved to such an extent that, by the early 1720's, the Governor of Astrakhan, A. P. Volynskii, attempted to convert the Kalmyks to Orthodoxy.

A full-scale tribal revolt, however, broke out shortly after Aiuka's death in 1724. Aiuka's widow, Darma Bala, proclaimed herself Khan, only to be challenged by her nephew, Donduk Ombo. Matters were complicated further when Volynskii recognized a tribal elder, Dorzhi Nazarov, as the new Khan, and other tribesmen supported another leader, Donduk Dashi. Tribal war continued over the next 15 years until, by 1741, only Donduk Dashi and Donduk Ombo's widow, Dzhana, were important contenders. Although the warfare was an internal tribal matter, the revolts interfered with Russian trade along the Volga. At first, the Russian Government used the military to quell the revolts. After the apparent failure of this policy, the College of Foreign Affairs created the Kalmyk Commission and assigned Tatishchev to find a way to restore peace in the Volga valley.

Tatishchev left St. Petersburg on 18 August 1742 and arrived in the Volga region by the end of October.[3] He reported to the College of Foreign Affairs from Saratov that he was discussing the Kalmyk situation with the local *voevoda*, Colonel Beklemishev. Tatishchev wrote that he expected to encounter great difficulties on the mission. Later, he held conferences with two military commanders, Generals Kol'tsov and Tarankov, who informed him that the fortresses along the Volga were in a ruinous condition, and that the one at Cheryni Iar was completely destroyed. It became apparent that Tatishchev could not rely upon the military to help him in his task.

Tatishchev's plan for ending the tribal warfare was personal and simple, quite similar to the one he had used earlier in settling the Bashkir revolts. He surmised that, if he could succeed in marrying Donduk Dashi to Dzhana, rivalry would cease and the Kalmyks would be united again.[4] He sent word to both Donduk Dashi and Dzhana to join him for a banquet. Although Dzhana did not attend the feast, her emissary said that she would consider the proposal. Donduk Dashi agreed to the marriage. Afterwards, Dzhana consented on the conditions that Tatishchev would use his influence to obtain fishing rights for the Kalmyks and would arrange to send her son Asar to St. Petersburg. With peace secured in the region, Tatishchev turned to the administrative tasks of the Commission.

On 27 December, Tatishchev wrote to Baron Ostermann to explain that the Kalmyk Commission faced many "unbelievably terrible" administrative problems.[5] He reported that he was carrying out an investigation of the fishing industry along the Volga. Tatishchev had promised Dzhana that he would obtain fishing rights for the Kalmyks; and, in all probability, he thought that a clear definition of these rights would settle the continuous disputes between the tribesmen and merchant fishermen. Tatishchev also took this opportunity to remind Ostermann of his long service to the State and to request transfer to other duties. He explained: "I am of no use here."

Tatishchev's statement that he was "of no use" in the Kalmyk Commission was merely a ploy. Within the next month, he worked out an agreement concerning fishing rights for both the Kalmyks and the merchant fishermen. After consultation with Colonel Beklemishev, he sent a preliminary report to the College of Foreign Affairs to describe the Volga fishing industry.

In the preliminary report, Tatishchev explained that fishing was the chief industry in the upper Volga region.[6] The Kalmyks depended upon fish for food, as well as for trading with merchant fishermen. The State maintained its own fishing industry, and had established offices in Saratov and in Astrakhan to lease fishing sites and to collect fees from merchant fishermen. Tatishchev reported, however, that the administration in these offices was in disorder and that the revenue obtained from the fishing fees was declining. Nevertheless, he thought that the industry had a great potential for increasing State revenue, if its administration were made more efficient. He argued that it was virtually impossible to insist on collecting fees from the Kalmyks, since they were nomadic and fished primarily for food. He closed the report by requesting that the College send geographers to map the Volga region so that the administration could have a better knowledge and control over the fishing areas.

After discussion with Donduk Dashi and the Kalmyk elders, Colonel Beklemishev, General Kunt'sov, and representatives of the merchant fishermen, on 14 January 1742, Tatishchev issued a proclamation which defined fishing rights in the Volga region.[7] The Kalmyks were permitted to fish on the Volga and its tributaries with tackle, and in the lakes near Saratov with nets, from October until the spring thaw. They could not use nets from June until October, and they had to use tackle when fishing for sturgeon. Merchant fishermen could not move into a site already occupied by Kalmyks. Although Tatishchev did not impose any

79

fee on Kalmyk catches, he held them subject to *obrok*[8] if a particular group remained in one locality for more than a year. Besides respecting Kalmyk rights, merchant fishermen had to keep records of and pay tithes on their catches. They could not make a catch closer than 18,000 feet from a previous one; and, as was the case for the Kalmyks, they had to use tackle when fishing for sturgeon. Kalmyk violations of these rules were to be reported to their Khan, whereas the merchant fishermen were dicretly responsible to the fishing offics in Saratov or Astrakhan.

Shortly thereafter, Tatishchev received word that he had been appointed Governor of Astrakhan. In November 1742, Peter the Great's daughter, Elizabeth, had been proclaimed Empress of Russia.[9] She immediatly dispatched one Captain Priklonskii to carry her personal greetings to Tatishchev. Later, on 15 December, she freed Tatishchev from the charges of the Golovkin Commission, restored his full salary as Privy Councilor, and appointed him Governor of Astrakhan.[10] Before leaving General Tarakanov in charge of the Commission, Tatishchev permitted the Kalmyks to settle on the western bank of the Volga. At this time, his son Evgraf joined him to assist him in his administrative tasks.

Although the area represented by Astrakhan Guberniia was annexed to Russia in the mid-sixteenth century, as late as Tatishchev's time much of the region was still unexplored and its administration poorly developed. Insurrections among the Tatars, Kirgiz, Kalmyks, and other nomadic tribes broke out sporadically within its borders. Externally, its governors had to keep close watch on political conditions in Persia, Daghestan, and Georgia, which bordered it on the south.

Astrakhan's location was ideal for Asian trade. The port of Astrakhan is situated on the Volga delta, and in the eighteenth century it was a center for European trade with Persia and Astrakhan. The Russian Empire exchanged fish, leather goods, linen, and European commodities for cottons and silks from Persia.[11] In the early 1740's, the English Company in Persia received permission to transport its goods overland through Astrakhan and the Russian Empire to London. In Tatishchev's time, Astrakhan Guberniia's population was a mélange of nomadic Asian tribes in the north and Russian, Armenian, Persian, Indian, and British merchants in the south. The port of Astrakhan was the administrative and military center of the guberniia.

If the political conditions in the bordering states and the sporadic tribal insurrections were not problems enough, Tatishchev found the administration of the Guberniia in total disorder when he assumed his new duties in February 1742. After completing an inspection tour, he reported to I. A. Cherkasov in St. Petersburg that he had found every-thing in a "ruinous condition."[12] Treasury records were inaccurate, and the population was so "dispersed" that he considered it an impossibility to administer effectively. He accused his predecessors of using incom-petents in the administration, and noted that their low salaries had encouraged embezzlement. Moreover, Tatishchev found the Guberniia's judicial processes almost non-existent. The administration was in such disorder that merchants did not bother to look to the Government for litigation or for protection from smuggling. In fact, smuggling, piracy on the Caspian Sea, and embezzlement were considered normal business procedures! At the close of his report, Tatishchev asked Cherkasov to explain these conditions to the Empress and to assure her that he would do his best to ameliorate them. Indeed, Tatishchev found his new assign-ment most discouraging. Undoubtedly, he longed for easier duties in Moscow or St. Petersburg. Within a year's time, he wrote to Cherkasov to report that he had not received his salary and to request transfer to another position.[13]

In spite of these difficulties, in less than three years Tatishchev accom-plished a great deal in making the administration more efficient and in strengthening the State's role in increasing commerce. For his first official act, he met with Persia's ruler, Nadir Shah, to arrange the trade of Astrakhan watermelons for Persian horses.[14] He also studied the possi-bilities of trading with Khiva and Bukhara over the Caspian Sea. In 1743, when an insurrection broke out against Nadir Shah in Persia, Tatishchev sought permission from the College of Foreign Affairs to allow the mer-chants of the various nationalities in the area to live in Astrakhan with full rights as Russian subjects. When the College denied permission, Tatishchev renewed the request during the following year. He thought that the Government could easily gain the respect of the merchants and strengthen the authority of the Guberniia's administration by grant-ing this permission.

Tatishchev had definite plans for increasing revenue from commerce and for encouraging industry in Astrakhan. He realized that the admin-istration was not effective enough to collect the existing taxes.[15] There-fore, he placed a tariff on all goods imported into Astrakhan, constructed customs houses, and established an inspection system to discourage smuggling. When he reported these measures to the College of Foreign Affairs, he was able to confirm that the new regulations he had imposed on merchant fishermen were already encouraging them to keep records of their catches. At the same time, he requested 30,000 rubles from the College to promote industry in the region and also requested permission to increase the quantity of wool imported from Persia.

In May 1745, Tatishchev proposed a new plan to increase industry in Astrakhan.[16] In short, he suggested that the Government should not collect taxes or inspect the records of the various weaving "factories" in the Guberniia for the next three years. Tatishchev explained that the Guberniia had many small "factories" in the sense that people spun and wove wool and cotton in their homes (cottage industry). Most of the weavers, he commented, did not know how to keep books, and traded with Armenian merchants on a day-to-day basis. Moreover, it was almost impossible to supervise these small units of production. Tatishchev's plan was a practical one. In all probability, he estimated, it would take him the three years to organize an efficient administration to carry out the supervision and to collect fees. More important, the declared respite from State interference would encourage production and new industry.

If poor administration and smuggling were among Tatishchev's greatest problems, revolution in Persia complicated matters even more. After Nadir Shah had crushed a series of insurrections in Persia, he crossed the Caucasus into Russian territory. At that point, Tatishchev discussed military preparations with Vice Governor Prince Mikhail Bariatinskii and Major General Prince Vladimir Dolgorukii.[17] Tatishchev persuaded Bariatinskii and Dolgorukii to postpone any military action against Nadir Shah. He pointed out that the army was not prepared for a campaign, and that Shah's absence would give rise to new revolts and compel him to return southwards. Tatishchev's reasoning proved correct. Shortly thereafter, insurrections broke out in Daghestan and Georgia, and Nadir Shah had to remove his troops from Russian soil.

Although peace was maintained between Russia and Persia, commercial rivalries remained intense. Russia had a great advantage in having a fleet on the Caspian Sea. In 1744, however, Nadir Shah began to build his own fleet of merchant-war vessels and threatened to deprive Russia and England of their monopoly of the Caspian trade.[18] Even more dangerous, Nadir Shah had employed John Elton, a representative of the English Company, to build the Persian ships.

In 1738, John Elton, who had served with Tatishchev in the Orenburg Expedition, represented the English Company in negotiations for permission for the Company to transport goods overland through the Russian Empire. Shortly thereafter, Elton established trading posts at Resht and Derbent to ship goods over the Caspian to the port of Astrakhan. At the same time, Elton agreed to build ships for the Russian Empire.

Elton, therefore, was employed by both the English Company and the Russian Empire.

In 1744, rumors reached Tatishchev and the College of Foreign Affairs that Elton was smuggling goods and, more important, building ships for Nadir Shah.[19] The College of Foreign Affairs complained about Elton to the English Company. The English Company thereupon sent another representative, Jonas Hanway, to investigate the charges made against Elton. From Hanway's account of the situation, there seems no doubt that the accusations against Elton were true. Hanway found the Company's records at Derbent and Resht in disorder, and Elton tried to prevent him from reporting this "unfavorable information" to their superiors in London. Moreover, Elton himself admitted to Hanway that he was building ships for Persia. However, he defended his activities on the grounds that he was doing so as a personal favor for Nadir Shah and that he was working for the best interests of the English Company. Naturally, the College of Foreign Affairs felt that Elton had betrayed their trust, since he had agreed to build ships for Russia. Then again, it is hard to see that Elton was acting in the best interests of the English Company when Persian ships would deny a monopoly of the Caspian trade to England—or, more correctly, to England and Russia. Obviously, Elton was acting in his own interests, and his indiscretion soured English-Russian relations in regard to the Caspian trade. Even though the English Company reprimanded Elton, in 1746 the College of Foreign Affairs prohibited the Company from transporting goods on the Caspian and confiscated their ships.[20] Elton died shortly thereafter.

While investigating Elton's activities, Hanway often met with the Governor of Astrakhan.[21] Hanway noted that he and Tatishchev discussed the latter's historical projects as well as ways of increasing trade in the region. He also observed that, while Tatishchev had accomplished a great deal in quieting rebellions among tribes in the region, "his genius turned most to literature and commerce; nor was he at all deficient in the arts of gain . . ."[22] Tatishchev must have been quite shrewd, since Hanway commented that he was particularly "rapacious" in dealing with Armenians.

Even in his practice of the "arts of gain," Tatishchev left a favorable impression on the Englishman. Hanway related that Tatishchev invited him to attend a large banquet. Tatishchev gave the feast on the occasion of the birth of his granddaughter.[23] When the guests arrived, they ". . . presented an offering, each according to his rank. This is a civil way of levying a heavy tax on the merchants, and a custom tho' not elegant, less absurd than that of some politer countries. . . ."[24] And Hanway observed, "This old man was remarkable for his socratical outlook, his emaciated body, which he preserved for many years by great temperance, and for keeping his mind continually employed."[25]

As Hanway mentioned, in spite of his almost insurmountable administrative tasks, Tatishchev did not neglect his interests in geography and history. He carried out a survey of Astrakhan Guberniia and sent 75 maps of the region to the Academy.[26] In 1744, he completed his "Introduction to an Historical and Geographical Description of the Great Russian Empire,"[27] which was an expanded version of the geographical sketch in the "Russia, or as it is Called Today, Rossiia." He also finished the first three parts (to the letter "K") of his *Geographical Lexicon*, in which he listed and described the various topographical features of the Empire.[28]

It seems that, at this time, someone in St. Petersburg had written to Tatishchev to suggest that he write a history of the reign of Peter the Great. In a letter to Cherkasov, Tatishchev explained that he was already too occupied with other historical and geographical writings, as well as with his overwhelming administrative duties, to begin another large project.[29] He also argued that he would need many assistants and substantial financial backing to gather sources. Indeed, Tatishchev was too busy to follow the suggestion. Such a project would not have appealed to him anyway. Tatishchev was more interested in the early history of Russia, and no doubt he would have offended some of his contemporaries with his own political outlook, which he certainly would have introduced into the work.

Tatishchev, however, did not forsake more acceptable opportunities to impress upon the Government his political ideas and the necessity for continuing Peter the Great's reforms. In 1743, when the Senate was in the process of discussing a new territorial division of the Empire, Tatishchev sent to St. Petersburg a "Memoir on the Forwarded Description of the Higher and Lower Government and Territorial Administration."[30] In the "Memoir," Tatishchev publicly criticized the "disorder" and incompetence on all administrative levels, and argued for general reforms. He attributed this condition to the lack of "political wisdom" on the Government's part. Good government and "political wisdom," he maintained, could be achieved only after a sense of community developed in the Russian Empire. Indeed, government, i.e., the monarchy, should be the ultimate source of authority in the Empire, but responsibility to that authority could only be attained through good administration and sound laws.

In addition to these criticisms, Tatishchev made several suggestions for reform. He suggested that the State tolerate all religions and promote education for all according to their station. The State must also foster trade and commerce in every possible way. Since, according to Tatishchev's formula, justice was the chief concern of government, the State must make every effort to reform its legal system. He pointed out that the then existing law codes were in disorder to the extent that some laws were contradictory to others. Moreover, justice was not uniform throughout the Empire. Tatishchev commented that the State had to enact a new law code so that an exact procedure for litigation and prosecution could be introduced throughout Russia. Finally, he observed that there was a great need for educated people in all levels of administration, and that a system of checks and supervision had to be established to ensure effective government. Through sound judicial and administrative procedures, the State would govern with "political wisdom" and succeed in generating a sense of community throughout the Empire.

Perhaps more significant, in his discussion of administration Tatishchev specifically addressed himself to the problem of the Russian nobility. He explained that the new rank system of Peter the Great had "purloined" from the Russian gentry their honor and their identification as a class. There were no provisions in the existing laws for distinguishing a nobleman from a non-nobleman except for the designations in service ranks. Tatishchev, therefore, suggested that the gentry conform to Peter's system and seek their social dignity in State service and through education. Moreover, their education would render the gentry immediate recognition, as well as prepare them for serving the State effectively and advancing the cultural position of Russia. In that way, the gentry would strengthen the Empire, as well as retain their honor and identity as a class.

Indeed, Tatishchev had mentioned these ideas concerning the nobility in his "Conversation" of 1733 and in his *Testament*. However, this was the first time that he had offered his solution to the problem in a formal document written to Government officials. There seems little doubt that he wanted his opinion on this subject made public.

Even though Tatishchev apparently had accomplished a great deal in increasing Russian authority in Astrakhan, he was relieved of his post in June 1745.[31] His removal, however, was not the result of action upon his earlier request of January 1743. It seems that individuals in St. Petersburg set out to discredit him, and established another commission to investigate new accusations of embezzlement. Moreover, Count A. P. Bestuzhev-Riumin in the College of Foreign Affairs had quarreled with Tatishchev's friend, Prince Nikita Trubetskoi. According to S. M. Solov'ev, Bestuzhev-Riumin thought that he could take revenge against

Trubetskoi by removing Tatishchev from State service. However this might be, the commission found Tatishchev guilty of embezzlement on 17 separate charges—several of which dated back to the Orenburg Commission—and "exiled" him to his estate at Boldino.

Tatishchev left Astrakhan in November 1745. On 27 December, he wrote Cherkasov to inform him that he would pass the winter at Tetiushi.[32] He explained that he was too ill to travel further in winter, and that he was discussing local problems with merchants and gentry in the area. Tatishchev then requested that Cherkasov help him return to State service so that he could work on plans for educational or judicial reforms. Unfortunately, Cherkasov was unable to help Tatishchev; and, in the following spring, he proceeded to his "exile."

During his last years in State service, Tatishchev became increasingly aware that the Empire had to reform in order to gain the respect of its inhabitants. Moreover, he recognized that the State had to play an active role in stimulating commerce and trade. Conditions in Astrakhan impressed upon him the necessity for good administration. The Kalmyks had greater respect for the Russian Empire when Tatishchev settled their dispute and delineated their fishing rights. When Governor of Astrakhan, he recognized that the merchants had little respect for Government because of administrative corruption. He therefore sought to reform the administration and intervene on behalf of the merchants.

From his experiences among the Bashkirs and Kalmyks, and as Governor of Astrakhan, Tatishchev felt compelled to voice his ideas on administrative reform to his superiors in St. Petersburg. Perhaps, too, he thought that the Government would be more receptive to his ideas with Peter the Great's daughter Elizabeth as the new Empress. Significantly, the "Memoir" he sent to the Senate did not dwell on the mechanics or on a particular aspect of reform. Instead, Tatishchev wanted to impress upon senators and others the necessity of continuing Peter the Great's policy of creating a Russian Government with its own goals and purposes. He thought that the Russian Empire could develop a genuine sense of community through good administration. Indeed, Tatishchev's activities in State service were his own personal fulfillment of his admonitions to his superiors to reform administration, draft a sound law code, and foster commerce and education. In a word, Tatishchev offered a formula for Russia to develop into a state unified by respect for law.

As he did in his *Testament*, Tatishchev assigned this important work to the nobility. Through their positions and responsibilities in State service, the Russian nobility could maintain their dignity and honor as a real, functional élite. As a class, the nobility were to lead in the creation of an efficient government. Tatishchev wanted the nobleman to function as a *Kulturträger* and bring Western European education to Russia in order to increase administrative efficiency, to glorify the State, and to give the Empire a sense of community.

In 1745, Tatishchev was approaching age 60. In ill health, he must have viewed his removal from duties in Astrakhan as a great relief. Nevertheless, Tatishchev by no means looked forward to an "exile" on his estate. Indeed, another would have welcomed this form of retirement after over 40 years of State service. But not Tatishchev. Embezzlement charges notwithstanding, Tatishchev still eagerly sought to serve the State in planning reforms which he thought were necessary, rather than to spend his last years in forced retirement.

Chapter XI

Retirement

Following his forced retirement from State service, V. N. Tatishchev spent his last years in "exile" on his estate at Boldino near Moscow. There he devoted most of his time to the intellectual pursuits which he had started nearly 30 years earlier. He often traded maps and manuscripts with members of the Academy of Sciences. He also corresponded with its President, K. G. Razumovskii, in hope that the Academy would publish his *Geographical Lexicon* and *Russian History* once they were completed. Since his request for reinstatement into State service had been denied, Tatishchev looked upon his geographical and historical research almost as a continuation of his duties as an administrator. Indeed, he thought that these projects would rank among his greatest contributions to fellow administrators and to posterity.

Although Tatishchev was no longer involved in State administration, he did make one final plea for reform during his retirement. In May 1748, he wrote to Count M. L. Vorontsov, the Empress' chamberlain, to ask him to deliver a project, "Presentation on Trade and Industry," to Elizabeth.[1] In the accompanying letter, Tatishchev explained that he wanted to impress upon the Empress the necessity of her doing everything possible to stimulate commerce and industry in Russia. Tatishchev divided his treatise into three parts. In the introduction, he compared Russia's situation to that of other European countries in regard to the needs of a national economy. Following the introduction, he wrote a historical essay in which he listed the accomplishments of several Russian monarchs in strengthening the country's commerce and industry. In this part, he was obviously suggesting to the Empress that she would be continuing the policies of her more illustrious predecessors by directly intervening in economic affairs. Tatishchev concluded the "Presentation" with suggestions which he thought would improve Russia's economic situation.

In the introduction, Tatishchev explained that commerce and industry were vital for any country. To illustrate his point, he attempted an analogy by likening industry to the stomach and commerce to the heart of the body of a state. He emphasized that a healthy economy produced wealth, which meant an increase in goods and services throughout the country. The wealth of a country, he maintained, should be enjoyed by both classes—the nobility and peasantry alike. Moreover, a healthy, strong economy made a state powerful not only through revenue obtained from its commerce, but also through self-sufficiency during war. Russia, he commented, covered a vast area and possessed many resources; and, therefore, it had great potential for wealth. Tatishchev, however, was quick to point out that he wanted Russia to develop an economy similar to that of England or France, and not like that of Spain, whose wealth was represented by a superficial accumulation of precious metals.[2]

In the historical essay, Tatishchev emphasized that, during Russia's past, several monarchs had acted personally to increase the country's wealth. He pointed that that, among Elizabeth's earliest predecessors, Oleg I, Igor I, and Vladimir I concluded trade agreements with Byzantium. Andrew Bogoliubskii made agreements with Emperor Frederick Barbarossa and invited architects to construct church in Vladimir. During the Tatar domination, the leaders of the city of Novgorod joined the Hanseatic League and enjoyed good trade connections with Lübeck and other commercial centers in Western Europe. Tsar Ivan the Great concluded commercial treaties with the Pope and the Holy Roman Emperor. Through these connections, he brought firearms and the invention of printing to Russia; he also invited foreign architects to beautify Moscow. His grandson Ivan the Terrible established trade connections with England, Holland, and Hamburg; and he sent emissaries to Italy, Grece, and Egypt. Tsar Alexis not only sought commercial ties with Western Europe; he founded Russia's metal industry. His son Peter the Great regarded commerce and industry of sufficient importance to create a special Mining and Manufacturing College. Peter also founded the Academy of Sciences to bring Western European education and art to Russia. Unfortunately, Tatishchev lamented, many of these accomplishments were destroyed during the reign of Peter II. Tatishchev then expressed the hope that Empress Elizabeth would continue, and build upon, her father's achievements.

Immediately following the essay, Tatishchev offered his suggestions to the Empress. He recommended that she, or the State, legislate codes for such business practices as property leasing and recognition of bankruptcy. He advised that she establish separate commissions for litigation of court cases involving businessmen and merchants, since most local officials were ignorant of commercial procedures. Tatishchev thought that the State should take a strong, active position in fostering trade and industry; that individual initiative on the part of merchants and industrialists was not sufficient to develop a strong economy in Russia. He therefore argued that the State should establish schools to provide commercial and language training for merchants and businessmen. He also recommended that the existing market be expanded and rationalized. The State should establish a bank to create credit and to make money readily available to entrepreneurs. Last, but not least, Tatishchev argued that the Empire neeeded a more orderly and efficient postal system, not only for the benefit of commerce but also for State affairs.

Tatishchev had two goals in mind when he wrote the "Presentation." First, the Empress, or the State, should take an active role in fostering a healthy economy and in increasing Russia's wealth. Thereby, the nation could grow more powerful and become self-sufficient in time of war. Second, and the more important motive for his writing the project, Tatishchev thought that the State could win the respect and loyalty of its subjects through its assumption of the responsibility for providing more goods and services, establishing schools for merchants, and legislating sound laws for commercial practices. No doubt, Tatishchev's reasoning was based upon his experiences as Governor of Astrakhan. There, the merchants had little respect for Government because of the local administrative disorder. The same situation could be applied to the entire Russian Empire. If the merchants throughout the Empire could be convinced of the benefits of good administration, sound laws, and the State's interest in their welfare, then they in turn would have greater respect for Government. Accordingly, the wealth generated in this process would soon benefit everyone in the Empire, and thereby all classes would have a genuine loyalty for the State and monarchy. In a word, Tatishchev wanted the Empress to foster a strong economy not only to increase the wealth of the Empire, but also to fulfill a necessary step in transforming Russia into a modern state.

Tatishchev's "Presentation" represents his last plea for reform. He seems to have preferred to concentrate all of his energies during his last years on continuing the research for his geographical and historical projects. In fact, following the completion of the first draft of his *Geographical Lexicon* in August 1746, he devoted his time almost exclusively to working on the *Russian History*.[3] His only other writing in geography during this period was a criticism of an unpublished manuscript by P. I. Rychkov.[4] Rychkov, who had served on the Orenburg Commission with Tatishchev, was preparing a description of the Tatars who lived in that region. In 1749, he sent the description to Tatishchev for criticism. In December, Tatishchev sent Rychkov a letter of praise and made several recommendations for improving the work.

In 1746, Tatishchev sent a completed first draft of the *Russian History* to the Academy of Sciences for publication.[5] The Academy, however, declined to publish it. For one thing, Tatishchev had written the first draft in a style approximating the language of his chronicle sources. It was long, unwieldy, and difficult to read. Moreover, the Academy at this time was more interested in publishing the works of the professional historians Gerhard Müller and Göttlieb Bayer.[6] Tatishchev, however, had already begun to prepare another draft of the *Russian History* written in a more contemporary style. Although the Academy was lukewarm about the new project, Razumovskii sent Tatishchev five assistants to help him complete the new revision.[7]

The following year, however, Tatishchev sought another means of publication. In 1747, he wrote to Jonas Hanway, the representative of the English Company whom he had met in Astrakhan, to ask him to present the *Russian History* to the Royal Society in London for publication.[8] In the letter, Tatishchev wrote that there had been no serious or complete accounts of the early history of the Russian Empire in any language. He also emphasized that the second part of the *Russian History*, i.e., from the calling of Riurik until the Tatar invasion, contained information about Norway, Sweden, and Hungary, ". . . which in the histories of those countries are either lost or transmitted down in a very dark manner."[9] If the Royal Society were interested, Tatishchev promised to send to it these two parts in a German translation, which they in turn could translate into English more easily than they could translate from the Russian. Unfortunately, Hanway did not help his Russian friend, because, in his own words, "that by no means suited my convenience."[10] With Hanway's refusal, Tatishchev probably had little hope that the *Russian History* would be published in his lifetime.

Tatishchev's *Russian History* is basically an objective account of events from the "very earliest times" until the election of Tsar Michael Romanov in 1613.[11] He divided the work into four parts in accordance with what he considered to be distinct periods in the development of the Russian State or monarchy. The first part is largely a description of the various peoples who lived in the Russian land prior to 860, when Gostomysl, the semi-legendary chief of the first known Russian dynasty, died. The second part begins with the calling of Riurik, the founder of the Riurikid dynasty, and ends with the Tatar invasion of the thirteenth century. The third period extends through the Tatar domination, a time when the monarchy lost its pre-eminence and when the grand princes of Muscovy were subservient to the Tatar khans. The fourth and final division begins with the re-establishment or reassertion of the authority of the Russian monarchy with the first Tsar, Ivan the Great. During this period, Russia prospered under "single rule" until the Time of Troubles.

Tatishchev noted that he had used over a thousand books in preparing the *Russian History*.[12] From time to time, he cited Ptolemy, Herodotus, Pliny, and Strabo among the ancients; and Bayle, Pufendorf, and Wolf among the moderns. For the most part, however, Tatishchev reconstructed events from Russian chronicles. He took great pains to include notes at the end of each chapter to explain variations or discrepancies in his sources. Sometimes, the notes are longer than the chapters themselves. In a word, Tatishchev made a great effort to arrive at the most accurate description of an event, and to include as much data as possible on a given situation.

Although the *Russian History* is largely a factual account, Tatishchev suggested his philosophy of history in the introduction, in three other chapters of the first part, and in the over-all organization of the work. Tatishchev considered Russian history to be an amalgam of geography, chronology, and genealogy, or an account of political geography over a period of time.[13] Thus, he presented an account of the events which transpired within the territory of the Russian Empire. In Russian history, the body politic was the monarchy, and therefore Tatishchev placed an emphasis on genealogy. According to his political theory outlined in the "Unrestrained and Concerted Discourse," the Russian land, being so vast and without natural borders, could be governed effectively only by a monarchy.[14]

Tatishchev clarified his philosophy in three chapters entitled: "On Geography in General and on Russian [Geography]," "Early Divisions of the Russians," and "On Early Rule and Others in Example."[15] In the first two, he accounted for eight divisions among the peoples who lived in the Russian land in early times similarly to what he did in his "Russia, or as it is Called Today, Rossiia." He thus showed that Russian history is not the history of one people or of one nation, but rather an account of many peoples who had inhabited in the past the area of the Russian Empire as it existed in Tatishchev's own time, or who then were inhabiting it. In "On Early Rule and Others in Example," Tatishchev explained that the monarchy had developed in Russia according to natural law, and he reiterated his arguments that single rule was the only reasonable form of government in the Russian land. The monarchy became the one symbol which united into a state those who lived in the Russian land.

Tatishchev's political ideas are apparent in the organization of the *Russian History*. He devoted the first part to a description of the various peoples who lived in the Russian land; he thereby inferred that Russia or the Russian Empire was made up of various "nations." It was impossible to speak of Russia as a nation, but rather as an empire composed of many smaller nations. Tatishchev divided the remainder of the work into three parts corresponding to periods in which the monarchy increased or decreased its authority. He then devoted a chapter to each monarch's reign. Tatishchev's organization, therefore, supports his theory that Russia was best governed by a monarchy, because only the monarch could unite the many nations into an empire.

His account of the origin of the Russian monarchy with the calling of Riurik illustrates this point best. At first glance, however, it appears that there is only a slight difference between his interpretation and that of the "Normanist School."[16] Tatishchev has been so misunderstood on this issue that Anatole G. Mazour claimed that he rejected the Norman Theory,[17] while Hans Rogger thought that he accepted it.[18] Actually, Tatishchev neither accepted nor rejected the Norman Theory in the sense which they implied, because the Norman and anti-Norman positions were not yet established at the time he wrote the *Russian History*. Although he included a chapter on Bayer's research in the work, his account was entirely his own.

According to Tatishchev, Riurik was not the first Russian monarch; prior to 860, the Russian land, or a significant part of it (around Novgorod), had been ruled by Gostomysl and his predecessors for at least five generations.[19] Gostomysl had four sons and three daughters. Since the sons had died at an early age, Gostomysl chose Riurik, son of his second daughter and the leader of the Varangian Rus, to succeed him upon his death. In 862, Riurik and his brothers came from the area now known as Finland to rule over the Russian land. Even though there are similarities between his account and the Norman Theory, Tatishchev was not interested in asserting the superiority or inferiority of the Rus over other peoples who dwelled in the Russian land. Most certainly, he did not view the theory as a fabrication of some "Germanic School," as M. V. Lomonosov did decades later. Tatishchev used the account of the calling of Riurik to demonstrate that Russia needed single rule and that its first form of government was monarchy. If his Varangians came from Finland, that was of little importance. They were among the many other peoples who had migrated and dwelled in the Russian land.

Whether Tatishchev has been interpreted as a Normanist or anti-Normanist, his *Russian History* has evoked more serious criticism over the past two centuries. His critics have focused on three issues. First, Tatishchev fabricated some sources and used others uncritically. Second, the *Russian History* lacks a philosophy of history, and is therefore of

93

little consequence in Russian historiography. And, third, Tatishchev failed to portray a "national consciousness" in the work.

The historian N. M. Karamzin,[20] at the beginning of the nineteenth century, and S. L. Peshtich,[21] today, have accused Tatishchev of inventing sources and of using others uncritically. Other historians, such as Gerhard Müller, M. N. Pogodin, and M. N. Tikhomirov, have defended Tatishchev against these accusations on the grounds that a source cannot be called "fictitious" because it is no longer available.[22] In fact, Müller published the *Russian History* in the eighteenth century, and Tikhomirov sponsored a new edition in the 1960's, precisely because it contains materials which have been either lost or destroyed. This dispute can be settled in only one of two ways: Either the lost sources will be found to vindicate Tatishchev, or his critics will have to demonstrate that he deliberately falsified evidence. And, in regard to his use of these sources, Tatishchev was no more and no less sophisticated, awkward, or inaccurate than were his contemporaries. To be sure, he was not a "professional historian," as were Müller and Bayer. Nevertheless, his gathering, assembling, and organizing of his sources into the most complete history of Russia up to his time were no small accomplishments.

In all probability, the criticism that Tatishchev's *Russian History* lacked a philosophical outlook grew out of a misunderstanding of the work and its author's purpose. In his article "Tatishchev's Interest in History," H. C. Schlieper stated that, although Tatishchev was aware of contemporary historical scholarship in the West, ". . . he chose to ignore it and settled on a format that was superficially different from that of traditional Russian historiography."[23] As already mentioned, Tatishchev indeed had a philosophy of history, and he organized his work according to a particular preconceived pattern. However, Schlieper's argument loses its validity on other grounds. Throughout his *Russian History*, Tatishchev continually referred to the writings of Bayle, Pufendorf, and Wolf, among other Western historians. Tatishchev, however, wanted to break from the tradition of writing a general history which expounded natural law. He felt his task was to present the concrete events of Russian history. In that sense, Tatishchev's *Russian History* can be compared with Bayle's *Dictionnaire*,[24] although Tatishchev's is, of course, a lesser work. Both Bayle and Tatishchev were interested in the accumulation of data. Although Tatishchev, in contrast to Bayle, organized his facts into a preconceived pattern, his *Russian History* can be interpreted as an expression of the trend away from deductive toward inductive reasoning which occurred in European philosophy in the eighteenth century. Rather than "ignoring" the scholarship of his contemporaries, it is more correct to say that Tatishchev, similar to Bayle, was among the first to "react" to it! Moreover, as the first attempt at a complete, critical, and "scientific" history of Russia, Tatishchev's *Russian History* can be considered the first step away from the chronicles in Russian historiography. In fact, it was Tatishchev who established the format for Russian historical writing, and for that reason he is rightfully called the "Father of Russian Historiography."

Hans Rogger's assertion that the *Russian History* failed to portray a "national consciousness" grew out of a similar misunderstanding.[25] No one could have been more conscious of the minorities problem in eighteenth century Russia than V. N. Tatishchev, and his *Russian History* reflected his awareness of the situation. Rogger's statement, however, obscured Tatishchev's meaning of Russian history or of Russian "nationalism." From his account of the "very earliest times," Tatishchev inferred that the history of Russian was one of several different peoples and cultures. He emphasized this situation when he proposed a new regional division in his "Russia, or as it is Called Today, Rossiia." During his career as an administrator in the frontier regions, Tatishchev came into contact with various peoples, all of whom he envisioned would be integrated into the Russian Empire. The Bashkirs, Kalmyks, and Tatars had little in common with the Great Russians; each people had its own language, customs, and "history." Tatishchev tried to gain their confidence for, and win their loyalty to, the Empire by explaining to them the advantages of Russian rule, its administration, justice, and commerce. The symbol, the one concrete image which all of these peoples could understand, was the monarchy. For example, when Tatishchev met with Kirgiz Khan Abul Hair, he compelled him to renew his oath to the Empress. When in Astrakhan, he prevented feuding among the Kalmyks by safeguarding their fishing rights. Tatishchev, therefore, in a sense recognized the problem of "national consciousness," and his *Russian History* views Russia as a nation that was developing into a community— an empire unified by respect for law and the symbol of monarchy. In short, Tatishchev believed that a continuation of the Petrine reforms would give all Russian subjects the sense of belonging to a unique community.

Tatishchev worked on his *Russian History* until a short time before he died in July 1750. On 13 July, two days before his death, he and his grandson Rostislav Evgrafievich traveled two miles on horseback to the village church.[26] After attending services, Tatishchev showed the priest and his grandson the family cemetery plots and told the grave diggers to prepare his final resting place. The next day, a courier arrived from

Empress Elizabeth to announce that she had freed him from exile and had awarded him the Order of Alexander Nevskii. Tatishchev thanked the Empress, but he declined the honor. Later, he confessed his sins and received the Sacrament in preparation for death.

Shortly before he expired on the 15th, Tatishchev called his son Evgraf and others to his bedside.[27] He reminded his son that he should follow the law of God, and "always be truthful and never obsessed with passions." Life holds many difficult times, he said, but one ". . . must be strong and patient in all misfortunes no matter how great they are." He told his son to serve the State with dignity, and he admonished him to live a simple life and to avoid luxuries: "Wealth is the origin of idleness, and idleness is the beginning of all evils." He then told Evgraf to teach his grandson Rostislav fear of the Lord, and to educate him for the good of the Fatherland and society. Finally, he reminded Evgraf to read the Bible often, especially the New Testament, and told him never to forget the importance of doing good works. His final words were:

> That is all, my dear son, that I want to say to you for the last time as is my duty. Now, I die with the satisfaction that my wish has been fulfilled. I ask you as a friend, and I command you as your father, to fulfill these [admonitions] exactly.[28]

During his retirement from State service, Tatishchev tried to fulfill the tasks which he outlined for the new Petrine nobleman in his *Testament*. He looked upon the writing of the *Russian History* as an extension of his work in State service. He wrote the *Geographical Lexicon* ostensibly to provide administrators and the gentry with information necessary for governing the Empire. He also made one last attempt to impress upon the Empress, in his "Presentation on Trade and Industry," the importance of the reforms which were necessary to stimulate the Russian economy. In a word, Tatishchev tried to share his erudition and experiences with his contemporaries in these writings; he took upon himself the task of *Kulturträger*.

Criticism notwithstanding, Tatishchev's *Russian History* indeed stands as a landmark in Russian historiography. He began the tradition of organizing material around the reigns of the individual monarchs. His method and his emphasis on the accumulation of data demonstrate that he was in tune with Western European historical scholarship. In fact, the *Russian History* is still used today as a source for material which has since been lost or destroyed. But Tatishchev had another purpose in mind when he wrote it. The *Russian History* portrays the Russian Empire as developing into a community unified by respect for law and by its monarchy—a cause which Tatishchev championed throughout his long career in State service.

Chapter XII

Conclusion: Tatishchev's Legacy

V. N. Tatishchev was one of the first noblemen in Russia to possess the new mentality created by the Petrine civil service. By the end of Peter the Great's reign, he had become totally committed to assisting the first Emperor in centralizing Russian government. Tatishchev was well suited for this role. He entered State service during his formative years, and had ample opportunity for personal contact with Peter the Great. No doubt, his having been in the presence of the Emperor greatly encouraged his loyalty to the monarchy and the Russian State. Perhaps just as important was Tatishchev's status as a member of the lower nobility. The new civil service system gave him the opportunity to use his education and administrative expertise to rise to the third highest rank in the Petrine Table of Ranks. Rather than defending the nobility's seventeenth century prerogatives, Tatishchev supported Peter the Great's service requirements and goals for Russia.

Tatishchev readily adjusted to the new demands made upon the Russian nobility. In fact, Peter the Great's system motivated him to become a successful administrator. In the years after the first Emperor's death, Tatishchev personally continued Peter the Great's program to rationalize the bureaucracy and to centralize the Russian government. Among his more important achievements, he established a strong State metal industry in the Ural Mountain region and headed administrations in Orenburg and Astrakhan during a pivotal period of imperial expansion into these newly added areas.

During his first years in State service, Tatishchev came to regard his offices as State trusts, and he made all of his decisions on the basis of how they strengthened the authority of the Russian Government and protected the dignity of the monarch. Tatishchev, to be sure, admitted in his *Testament* that he had accepted bribes for some of his decisions. Nevertheless, he was quick to point out that his bribe taking in no way interfered with justice, and that it actually increased administrative efficiency. In fact, when Tatishchev explained the accusations against him to Peter the Great, Peter recognized Tatishchev's loyalty to the State despite his bribe taking. The important point, however, is that Tatishchev continually kept in mind his goal of administrative efficiency.

Tatishchev's outlook toward the Russian State was not limited to the bureaucracy and administration per se. By the eighteenth century, the Empire had extended its rule over peoples who did not share the language, culture, and traditions of Muscovy; and Tatishchev's experiences on the frontier impressed upon him that Russia was a multinational state. He became convinced that the only way the Empire could win the respect and loyalty of these newly added peoples was through education, sound laws, and good administration. Tatishchev used his position to advance these principles whenever possible. As administrator of the Urals factory complex, he proposed for his region the first program of State education for all classes in Russia. On numerous occasions, he argued for a reform of the law code, and when in charge of the Orenburg and Kalmyk Commissions, he gained the respect of the local tribes for the Empire by convincing them of the benefits of Russian rule and administration. Tatishchev's experiences in the civil service continually renewed his conviction of the importance of completing Peter the Great's work of transforming Russia into a country ruled through respect for law.

Monarchy had a definite and important role in Tatishchev's scheme. According to his political theory, only a monarchy could effectively govern the vast area of the Russian Empire and symbolize the unity of all its subjects. Moreover, Tatishchev was impressed by the rapid progress Russia had made toward becoming a modern state under the firm rule of Peter the Great. Therefore, when the majority of the nobles wanted to slow down the pace of the Petrine reforms, and plotted to establish an oligarchic or aristocratic government in Russia in 1730, Tatishchev supported the preservation of the monarchy. During the first stage of the succession crisis, he submitted to the nobles a project, "An Unrestrained and Concerted Discourse," in which he defended the powers of the monarch and argued for the continuation of Peter the Great's service requirements. When it became apparent later that the oligarchic party and the nobility were succeeding in their attempts to deprive the monarchy of its traditional authority, Tatishchev helped organize a palace revolution which restored the autocracy in Russia. It was Tatishchev's mentality as a Petrine civil servant that motivated him to preserve the monarchy.

Although Tatishchev supported the monarchy and the continuation of the Petrine reforms during the succession crisis, he also understood the problems which confronted the nobility as a class in the first half of the eighteenth century. He realized that the Petrine reforms and Table of Ranks had deprived the nobility of their traditional social prerogatives and forced them to serve in an impersonal bureaucracy. Tatishchev believed that the nobility should follow his example and work for the modernization of Russia. Thereby they could adjust to their new obligations and regain their social status by acquiring the education and culture which their service requirements demanded of them. Tatishchev offered this solution to the nobility in his "Unrestrained and Concerted Discourse" when he assigned to them the task of enlightening Russia. He argued the issue again in the "Conversation" of 1733 and in his *Testament*. In short, Tatishchev wanted the nobility to remain an élite, but now in the new Petrine sense; the Russian nobleman then could be identified by his responsibility as a *Kulturträger* who assisted the monarch in administering the State.

Tatishchev himself assumed the role of a *Kulturträger* and contributed greatly to the enlightening of Russia. He encouraged education and the spread of knowledge and wrote the "Conversation" of 1733 to acquaint his son—and, undoubtedly, others—with some of the major philosophers of Western Europe. He tried to offer the nobility a solution to their social dislocation in his *Testament*. He encouraged the publication of the first atlas of the Russian Empire, and drew upon his geographical and historical knowledge to compile a *Geographical Lexicon* and to offer a regional reform project to the Senate. Last, but not least, he wrote his *Russian History* to make available to the nobility and civil administrators a knowledge of the Empire's past.

Even more important, Tatishchev's *Russian History* reflects his attitude toward the Russian State. Since he believed that autocracy was the only workable form of government for Russia, he divided his chapters according to the reigns of the various monarchs. Accordingly, he sought to demonstrate that only monarchy could effectively unify the vast area and various peoples of the Empire into a state. Tatishchev, therefore, was very conscious of the nationalities problem that Russia faced as the Empire expanded eastward. Thus, Tatishchev's *Russian History* portrays the development of the Russian Empire as the growth of a multinational state unified by monarchy and respect for law. *16 8397*

Historians have rightfully considered Tatishchev the "Father of Russian Historiography," because his *Russian History* was the first scientific survey of Russia's past. However, Tatishchev has merited the distinction on still other grounds. First, it was Tatishchev—not Göttlieb Bayer—who introduced the data of the controversial Norman Theory into Russian historiography. Second, it was Tatishchev who brought the most advanced rationalist historiographical scholarship to Russia by placing emphasis on the accumulation of data, similar to the way Pierre Bayle compiled his *Dictionnaire*.

The heritage from V. N. Tatishchev is great. He played an important role in the preservation of the autocracy during the succession crisis of 1730. As an administrator, he headed the Urals factory system and established the Empire's authority in the frontier regions during a critical period of Russia's growth. However, he shared with the nobility his ideas on the problems that confronted them as a class in the years immediately following the Petrine reforms. Although it is impossible to measure Tatishchev's direct influence on this issue, if nothing else, his writings bear witness to the transformation of the nobility in the first half of the eighteenth century. And the *Russian History* is a monument of scientific historical writing in Russian historiography. Through his rich political and cultural legacy, V. N. Tatishchev was indeed a "Guardian of the Petrine Revolution."

Notes

CHAPTER I

1. For a convenient survey of the Petrine era in the English language, see L. Jay Oliva, *Russia in the Era of Peter the Great*, (Englewood Cliffs, N. J.: Prentice-Hall, Inc., 1969).

2. For an excellent account of the Petrine Church reform, see James Cracraft, *The Church Reform of Peter the Great*, (Stanford, Calif.: Stanford University Press, 1971).

3. On the Petrine civil service, see Simone Blanc, "La Pratique de l'Administration Russe dans la Première Moitié du XVIIIe Siècle," *Revue d'Histoire Moderne et Contemporaine*, X (1963), 45-64. For recent studies on the eighteenth century Russian nobility, see Antony Lentin, "The Russian Nobility in the First Third of the Eighteenth Century, in M. M. Shcherbatov, *On the Corruption of Morals in Russia*, edited and translated by Antony Lentin (Cambridge: Cambridge University Press, 1969), pp. 9-15; Michael Confino, *Domaines et Seigneurs en Russie vers la Fin du XVIIIe Siècle: Etude de Structures Agraires et de Mentalités Economiques* (Paris: Institut d'Etudes Slaves de l'Université de Paris, 1963), pp. 20-69; and Marc Raeff, Origins of the Russian Intelligentsia, (New York: Harcourt, Brace & World, Inc., 1966). For a description of Russian society before the Petrine reforms, see Reinhard Wittram, *Peter I: Czar und Kaiser* (2 vols.; Göttingen, Vandenhoeck & Ruprecht, 1964), I, pp. 21-79.

4. V. N. Tatishchev, "Razgover dvukh priatelei o pol'ze nauk i uchilishch," edited by N. A. Popov, *Chteniia v imperatorskom obshchestve istorii i drevnostei rossiskikh pri moskovskom universitete*, I (1887), pp. 1-171.

5. V. N. Tatishchev, *Dukhovanaiia tainago sovetnika, i astrakhanskago gubernatora Vasiliia Nikiticha Tatishcheva*, (St. Petersburg: 1773).

6. V. N. Tatishchev, *Leksiken ressiskoi, istoricheskoi, geograficheskoi, politicheskoi, i grazhdanskoi, sochinennyi gospodinem tainym sovetnikom i astrakhanskim gubernatorum Vasil'em Nikitichem Tatishchevym*, (3 vols.; St. Petersburg: Gornyi Uchilishch, 1793).

7. V. N. Tatishchev, *Istoriia rossiiskaia v semi tomakh*, edited by A. I. Andreev, S. N. Valk, and M. N. Tikhomirov, (7 vols.: Leningrad-Moscow: Izdatel'stvo Akademii Nauk SSSR and Izdatel'stvo "Nauk," 1962, 1963, 1964, 1965, 1966, and 1968.).

CHAPTER II

1. Popov, *Tatishchev*, pp. 532-533, n. 1; and S. S. Tatishchev, *Rod Tatishchevykh 1400–1900* (St. Petersburg: 1900), p. 65.

2. A *voevoda* was a provincial governor.

3. Bestuzhev-Riumin, *op. cit.*, p. 5.

4. Tatishchev, *Dukhovanaiia*, p. 27. Tatishchev wrote this "testament" or will as a moral guide for his son Evgraf in 1740. At the time, Tatishchev was imprisoned, and he thought that he was going to die. See Chapter IX.

5. E. E. Kolosov, "Novye biograficheskie materialy o V. N. Tatishcheve," *Arkheograficheskii ezhegodnik za 1963 god* (1964), pp. 107-108. Kolosov's research is based entirely on sources in the Arkhiv Artilleriiskii-istoricheskii Muzeii.

6. Popov, Tatishchev, p. 14.

7. Prince Igor was killed in 945 when trying to exact tribute from the Derevliane. His wife Olga sought to avenge him.

8. Grau, *op. cit.*, p. 20.

9. Kolosov, *op. cit.*, p. 110.

10. Grau, *op. cit.*, pp. 22-23.

11. Tatishchev, *Istoriia rossiiskaia v semi tomakh*, I, p. 149. Tatishchev's *Russian History* contains some biographical information.

12. Kolosov, *op. cit.*, p. 110.

13. Grau, *op. cit.*, pp. 22-23.

14. Kolosov, *op. cit.*, p. 110.

15. *Ibid.*, p. 109; Bestuzhev-Riumin, *op. cit.*, pp. 6-7; and Grau, *op. cit.*, p. 24.

16. Eduard Winter, *Halle als Ausgangspunkt der Deutschen Russlandkunde in 18. Jahrhundert* (Berlin: Akademie-Verlag, 1953), pp. 82-84.

17. Kolosov, *op. cit.*, p. 110.

18. *Ibid.;* and Grau, *op. cit.*, pp. 25-26.

19. A portion of the letter is printed in Grau, *op. cit.*, p. 25.

20. Tatishchev, *Istoriia rossiiskaia v semi tomakh*, I, 87-88.

21. *Ibid.*, p. 88.

22. This same scene was chosen by V. O. Kliuchevskii to describe Peter the Great's character. Kliuchevskii, however, said that an eyewitness "apparently" told Tatishchev about what took place in 1717. Kliuchevskii's doubt is not necessary, since there is ample evidence that Tatishchev was in Peter the Great's presence many times during that year. Moreover, Tatishchev's description reads as if he were the eyewitness. Perhaps Kliuchevskii's reservation was due to the lack of information concerning Tatishchev in the nineteenth century. See V. O. Kliuchevskii, *Kurs ruskoi istorii*, IV (Moscow: Gosudarstvennoe Sotsial'no-Ekonomicheskoe Izdatel'stvo, 1937), 44.

23. Kolosov, *op. cit.*, p. 112.

24. *Polnoe sobranie zakonov Rossiiskoi Imperii s 1649 goda* (45 vols.; St. Petersburg: 1830), V, 525, No. 3128 for 11 December 1717; and 528, No. 3133 for 15 December 1717. (Hereafter cited *PSZ*.) See also Ellinor von Puttkamer, "Einflusse Schwedischen Rechts auf die Reformen Peters des Grossen," *Zeitschrift fur Auslandisches offentliches Recht und Volkerrecht*, XIX (Aug.-Nov. 1958), 378-379.

25. Kolosov, *op. cit.*, p. 113.

26. S. A. Feigina, *Alandskii kongress* (Moscow: Izdatel'stvo Akademii Nauk SSSR, 1959), p. 207; and Tatishchev, *Istoriia rossiiskaia v semi tomakh*, I, 88.

27. The text of the project is printed in P. P. Pekarskii, "Novyia izvestiia o V. N. Tatishcheve," *Zapiski Imperatorskoi Akademii Nauk*, IV (1864), 8–10.

28. Tatishchev, *Istoriia rossiiskaia v semi tomakh*, I, 89.

29. Letter of 1726 to I. A. Cherkasov, printed in Pekarskii, *op. cit.*, p. 11.

30. M. A. Gorlovskii, "K istorii osnovaniia Ekaterinburga," *Istoricheskie zapiski*, XXXIX (1952), 159-180.

31. *Istoricheskii ocherk i obzor fondov rukopisnogo otdela biblioteki Akademii Nauk*, II (Leningrad-Moscow: Izdatel'stvo Akademii Nauk SSSR, 1958), 226.

32. B. B. Kafengauz, "Stroitel'stvo pervykh ural'skikh zavodov," *Voprosy istorii*, V-VI (1945), 50ff. See also Roger Portal, *L'Oural au XVIIIᵉ Siècle: Etude d'Histoire Economique et Sociale* (Paris: Institut d'Etudes Slaves de l'Université de Paris, 1950), pp. 52-64.

33. Portal, *op. cit.*, pp. 52-54.

34. *Ibid.*, pp. 58 and 64.

35. N. I. Pavlenko, *Istoriia metallurgii v Rossii XVIII veka* (Moscow: Izdatel'stvo Akademii Nauk SSSR, 1962), pp. 73-74; and B. B. Kafengauz, *Istoriia khoziaistva Demidovykh v XVIII-XIXvv*, I (Leningrad-Moscow: Izdatel'stvo Akademii Nauk SSSR, 1949), 153-166.

36. Kafengauz, "Stroitel'stvo," pp. 70ff.

37. *Ibid.*, p. 74.

38. Gorlovskii, *op. cit.*, p. 159.

39. *Ibid.*, pp. 160-161.

40. A *verst* is 3500 American feet.

41. Gorlovskii, *op. cit.*, p. 162.

42. Sverdlovsk today.

43. Gorlovskii, *op. cit.*, p. 161.

44. *Ibid.*, pp. 162-163.

45. *Ibid.*, pp. 165-166.

46. *Ibid.*, pp. 166-167.

47. *Ibid.*

48. Popov, *Tatishchev*, p. 37.

49. Grau, *op. cit.*, pp. 38-39; and Kafengauz, *Istoriia*, p. 164.

50. Popov, *Tatishchev*, pp. 37-38.

51. Gorlovskii, *op. cit.*, pp. 167-168; and Bestuzhev-Riumin, *op. cit.*, pp. 13-14.

52. Bestuzhev-Riumin, *op. cit.*, p. 16; and Tatishchev, *Istoriia rossiiskaia v semi tomakh*, I, 349.

53. Gorlovskii, *op. cit.*, p. 173. Parts of the letter are quoted.

54. *Ibid.*

55. *Ibid.*, pp. 172-174.

56. Bestuzhev-Riumin, *op. cit.*, pp. 13-14.

57. V. N. Tatishchev, *The Testament of Basil Tatishchev*, translated by John Martinof (Paris: Benjamin Duprat, 1860), pp. 26-27. Although Martinof's translation is incomplete, he successfully preserved the literary style of the document.

58. *Ibid.*, p. 40.

59. Tatishchev, *Istoriia rossiiskaia v semi tomakh*, I, 89.

60. *Ibid.*, p. 84.

61. *Ibid.*, p. 349.

62. Tatishchev, *Testament*, p. 27.

CHAPTER III

1. Popov, *Tatishchev*, p. 54.

2. *Ibid.*

3. The rank of Collegial Counselor was the sixth in the Petrine Table of Ranks; it made Tatishchev a governing official in the College of Mines and Manufactures.

4. Popov, *Tatishchev*, p. 537, n. 26.

5. *Ibid.*, p. 54.

6. Pekarskii, *op. cit.*, p. 13. Pekarskii's article is primarily a collection of Tatishchev's letters and other documents found in the Cabinet papers of Peter the Great. On 23 October 1724, Tatishchev held a conversation with Count F. W. Burgholz in which he told the Count that Peter the Great was sending him to Sweden for some "secret affairs" besides the official reasons for his mission. In all likelihood, his "observations" of the Swedish Government, an order which was not included among Peter's decrees, were the nature of his secret task. See "Geschichte der Familie der Grossfürstin und Regentin Anna und der Herzogs Anton Ulrich von Braunschweig," *Büschings Magazin*, XXII (1788), 495.

7. Pekarskii, *op. cit.*, p. 17.

8. Popov, *Tatishchev*, p. 59-60. Parts of the letter are quoted.

9. *Ibid.*

10. Pekarskii, *op. cit.*, p. 14, Tatishchev to Cherkasov, letter of 18 December 1724. Cherkasov was private secretary to Empress Elizabeth.

11. *Ibid.*, p. 16, Tatishchev to Cherkasov, letter of 2 January 1725.

12. *Ibid.*, pp. 16-17, Tatishchev to Empress Catherine, letter of 9 April 1725.

13. *Ibid.*, p. 15.

14. *Ibid.*, p. 19.

15. *Ibid.*, pp. 17-18, Tatishchev to Cherkasov, letter of 9 April 1725.

16. *Ibid.*, pp. 20-22, Tatishchev to Cherkasov, letter of 14 May 1725.

17. *Ibid.*, p. 22, Tatishchev to Cherkasov, letter of 25 June 1725.

18. *Ibid.*, pp. 22-23.

19. Riurik is usually placed in the ninth century.

20. Björner's notes are included in Tatishchev's list of expenses. Pekarskii, *op. cit.*, p. 28.

21. *Ibid.*, pp. 25-26, Tatishchev to Cherkasov, letter of 1725.

22. Popov, *Tatishchev*, pp. 63-64.

23. Pekarskii, *op. cit.*, pp. 27-28. List printed.

24. *Ibid.*, pp. 29-30.

25. The most complete account of the Norman Theory in English is Alexander V. Riasanovsky, "Norman Theory of the Origin of the Russian State" (unpublished Ph.D. dissertation, Department of History, Stanford University, 1960). See also Nicholas V. Riasanovsky, "The Norman Theory of the Origin of the Russian State," *The Russian Review*, VII (1947), 96-110. For the present Soviet interpretation, see I. P. Shaskol'skii, *Normanskaia teoria v sovremennoi burzhuaznoi nauke* (Leningrad: Izdatel'stvo "Nauk," 1965).

26. For the beginnings of the Norman Theory as a nationalist issue, see Hans Rogger, *National Consciousness in Eighteenth Century Russia* (Cambridge: Harvard University Press, 1960), pp. 207-210.

27. Winter, *op. cit.*, p. 194.

28. See Chapter XI.

CHAPTER IV

1. Raeff, *Russian Intelligentsia*, pp. 81-82. See also S. M. Solov'ev, *Istoriia Rossii s drevneishikh vremen*, Book IX, Vol. 18 (Moscow: Izdatel'stvo Sotsial'no-Ekonomicheskoi Literatury, 1963), pp. 554ff.

2. The following essay is based on the accounts in Solov'ev, *Istoriia Rossii*, Book IX, Vol. 18, pp. 450-620, and Book X, Vol. 19, pp. 7-83; in Michael T. Florinsky, *Russia: A History and an Interpretation* (New York: The Macmillan Company, 1953), I, 432-440; and in Christoff von Manstein, *Memoirs of Russia* (London: Becket and De Hondt, 1770), pp. 1-25.

3. *PSZ*, VI, 496-497, No. 3893 for 5 February 1722.

4. Manstein, *op. cit.*, p. 2.

5. *Ibid.*, p. 13.

6. *Ibid.*, pp. 6-7.

7. Peter the Great had a strained relationship with his son Alexis. In 1718, there were rumors of a conspiracy to dethrone Peter and elevate Alexis in his place. Peter imprisoned his son and had him tortured to death. Menshikov was present at the torture sessions.

8. Manstein, *op. cit.*, p. 21.

9. *Ibid.*, pp. 22-23.

10. *Ibid.*, p. 23.

11. Peter the Great founded the Academy of Sciences and an accompanying university upon the suggestion of the German philosopher Göttfried Wilhelm Leibniz. The Academy attracted some of the best minds of Europe to Russia, creating the anomaly of an institution of the highest academic level in a country where illiteracy abounded. In a conversation with Peter the Great and the first president of the Academy, L. L. Blümentrost, in 1724, Tatishchev said that the establishment of the Academy was like a landowner's constructing a mill first and then digging a canal to supply the water to turn it. Tatishchev

preferred the introduction of a system of elementary education, the canal to supply the water to turn the mill in his analogy. See Tatishchev's letter to J. D. Schumacher, V. N. Tatishchev, "Perepiska V. N. Tatishcheva za 1746-1750gg," edited by A. I. Andreev, *Istoricheskii arkhiv*, VI (1951), 261-262.

12. The term "Learned Guard" was first used in the satire, "Theofan Arkhiepskop Novgorodskii 'k avtoru satiry,'" written by Prokopovich to Prince A. D. Kantemir. See Theofan [Prokopovich], Archbishop of Novgorod, *Sochineniia* (Leningrad-Moscow: Izdatel'stvo Akademii Nauk SSSR, 1961), pp. 216-217. The term "*druzhina*" has particular historical significance; the *druzhina* was in the retinue of the early Kievan princes. Two articles have been written on the Learned Guard. Although they concentrate on the Guard's absolutist political philosophy, both fail to describe the part it played in the succession crisis of 1730. See P. P. Epifanov, "'Uchenaia druzhina' i prosvetitel'stvo XVIII veka," *Voprosy istorii*, III (March 1963), 37-53; and G. V. Plekhanov, *Istoriia ruskoi obshchestvennoi mysli*, II (Moscow: Tvorchestvo "Mir," 1918), 98-160.

13. I. A. Chistovich, *Theofan Prokopovich i ego vremia* (St. Petersburg: Izdanie Imperatorskoi Akademii Nauk, 1868), pp. 1-23.

14. Theofan, *Sochineniia*, pp. 229-334 and 147-208.

15. G. A. Gukovskii, *Russkaia literatura XVIII veka* (Moscow: Gosudarstvennoe Uchebno-Pedagogicheskoi Izdatel'stvo, 1939), pp. 16-17.

16. "Slovo o vlasti i chesti tsarskoi," in Theofan, *Sochineniia*, pp. 76-93. The *Sermon* has been translated by Horace Lunt in Marc Raeff, ed., *Russian Intellectual History: An Anthology* (New York: Harcourt, Brace & World, Inc., 1966), pp. 14-30.

17. Raeff, *Intellectual History*, p. 16.

18. *Ibid.*, pp. 19-20.

19. *Ibid.*, p. 23.

20. *Ibid.*, p. 28.

21. *Ibid.*, p. 29.

22. Theofan [Prokopovich], Archbishop of Novgorod, "Pravda voli monarshei" in *PSZ*, VI, 602-643, No. 4870 for 21 April 1726.

23. Theofan [Prokopovich], Archbishop of Novgorod, "Dukhovnyi reglament" in *PSZ*, VI, 314-346, No. 3718 for 25 January 1721.

24. Solov'ev, *Istoriia Rossii*, Book IX, Vol. 18, pp. 608-699.

25. Chistovich, *op. cit.*, pp. 195-204.

26. Solov'ev, *Istoriia Rossii*, Book X, Vol. 19, p. 106.

27. Theofan, *Sochineniia*, pp. 216-217.

28. See Chapter V.

29. M. I. Radovskii, *Antiokh Kantemir i peterburskaia Akademiia Nauk* (Leningrad-Moscow: Izdatel'stvo Akademii Nauk SSSR, 1959), pp. 4-9.

30. *Ibid.*, pp. 9-15 and 25.

31. "Na khuliashchikh ucheniia" in A. D. Kantemir, *Sobranie stikhotvorenii* (Leningrad: Sovetskii Pisatel', 1956), pp. 57-62. For an analysis of Kantemir's early satires, see "Pervye gody literaturnoi deiatel'nosti Antiokha Kantemira"

in P. I. Berkov, *Problemy russkogo prosveshcheniia v literature XVIII veka* (Leningrad-Moscow: Izdatel'stvo Akademii Nauk SSSR, 1961), pp. 190-220.

32. "Na zavist' i gordost' dvorian zlonravnykh" in Kantemir, *op. cit.*, pp. 68-70.

33. "Petrida," *ibid.*, pp. 241-247.

34. Radovskii, *op. cit.*, pp. 20–21; Plekhanov, *Istoriia*, p. 155.

35. See Chapter V.

36. Radovskii, *op. cit.*, pp. 39-48.

37. *Ibid.*, pp. 48-62; see also F. Ia. Priimy, "Antiokh Dmitrievich Kantemir" in Kantemir, *op. cit.*, pp. 22-23.

38. Robert Shackleton, *Montesquieu: A Critical Biography* (Oxford: Oxford University Press, 1961), p. 176.

39. Radovskii, *op. cit.*, p. 56.

40. Tatishchev, *Istoriia rossiiskaia v semi tomakh*, I, 349; see also Grau, *op. cit.*, p. 116.

41. *PSZ*, VII, 859-860, No. 5156 for 18 September 1727.

42. Grau, *op. cit.*, pp. 143-144; and Winter, *op. cit.*, p. 188.

43. Grau, *op. cit.*, p. 142; and I. N. Koblens, *Andrei Ivanovich Bogdanov* (Moscow: Izdatel'stvo Akademii Nauk SSSR, 1958), pp. 123-124.

44. Winter, *op. cit.*, p. 194. See also Chapter II.

CHAPTER V

1. Korsakov's, the most complete account of the succession crisis, has been used extensively in the preparation of this chapter. D. A. Korsakov, *Votsarenie imperatritsy Anny Ioannovny* (Kazan: Imperatorskii Kazanskii Universitet, 1880).

2. The "Conditions" have been published in Korsakov, *Votsarenie*, pp. 17-18. Raeff has translated them into English: see Marc Raeff, ed., *Plans for Political Reform in Imperial Russia, 1700–1905* (Englewood Cliffs, N. J.: Prentice-Hall, Inc., 1966), pp. 45-46. Some historians think that Golitsyn intended to establish a constitutional regime in Russia similar to the one which existed in Sweden at that time; for this controversy, see Pavel Miliukov, *Iz istorii russkoi intelligentsii* (St. Petersburg: Tipografiia Montvid, 1903), pp. 1-51.

3. Manstein, *op. cit.*, p. 30.

4. Korsakov, *Votsarenie*, Appendix, pp. 9-11; Raeff, *Political Reform*, pp. 46-48.

5. Raeff, *Political Reform*, pp. 48-49.

6. V. N. Tatishchev, "Proizvol'noe i soglasnoe razsuzhdenie i mnenie sobravshagosia shliakhtstva russkago o pravlenii gosudarstvennon," *Utro*, 1859, pp. 369-379. A similar essay and expansion of Tatishchev's ideas can be found in his *Istoriia rossiiskaia v semi tomakh*, I, 359-370. Summaries of Tatishchev's political ideas can be found in Thornton Anderson, *Russian Political Thought* (Ithaca, N. Y.: Cornell University Press, 1967), pp. 133-136; and in S. V.

Utechin, *Russian Political Thought* (New York: Frederick A. Praeger Co., Inc., 1963), pp. 48-51.

7. Tatishchev was a student of Pufendorf's principles of natural law. He thought that the monarch should be chosen only by agreement with all the people.

8. "Monarchy" and "autocracy" were interchangeable terms for Tatishchev.

9. For the reader's convenience, the division of these items differs slightly from Tatishchev's original presentation.

10. Tatishchev here is inferring that the monarch is not liable to judgment by his subjects.

11. There is a confusion of dates in the manuscript: Tatishchev said that this group met on the 23rd and on the following day (i.e., the 24th) asked Anne to assume autocratic powers. He obviously meant the 24th and 25th, respectively. See Tatishchev, "Proizvol'noe i soglasnoe razsuzhdenie," p. 378.

12. Korsakov, *Votsarenie,* pp. 268-276; Tatishchev, "Proizvol'noe i soglasnoe razsuzhdenie," pp. 378-379.

13. Korsakov, *Votsarenie,* pp. 271-272; Raeff, *Political Reform,* pp. 50-51.

14. In all likelihood, this was the project drafted by Kantemir the evening before; it is hardly possible that such an explicit declaration could have been written at the height of the confusion in the Kremlin. Korsakov, *Votsarenie,* pp. 275-276; Raeff, *Political Reform,* pp. 51-52; and Tatishchev, "Proizvol'noe i soglasnoe razsuzhdenie," p. 378.

15. This quote is taken from Raeff's translation, *Political Reform,* p. 52.

16. Manstein, *op. cit.,* p. 35.

17. Popov, *Tatishchev,* pp. 114-130.

18. Korsakov, *Votsarenie,* p. 191.

19. Raeff, *Political Reform,* p. 44.

20. G. A. Protasov, "Zapiska Tatishcheva o 'Proizvol'nom razsuzhdenii' dvorianstva v sobytiiakh 1730g," *Problemy istochnikovedeniia,* XI (1963), 237-265.

21. *Ibid.,* p. 257.

22. In the first chapter of *The Philosophy of the Enlightenment,* Ernst Cassirer has noted the following characteristics of the eighteenth century Enlightenment: use of analysis and, particularly, the method of induction; analysis applied to psychological and sociological problems; unity in nature and history; possession of known goals; the ideal of intellectual progress; the belief in the immutability of reason. Ernst Cassirer, *The Philosophy of the Enlightenment,* translated by Fritz Koelln and James Pettegrove (Princeton: Princeton University Press, 1951), pp. 3-36.

23. Charles Louis de Secondat Montesquieu, *L'Esprit des Loi* (Paris: Garnier Frères, n.d.), III, VIII, XV, and XVIII.

24. Shackleton, *op. cit.,* pp. 228-240.

25. Carl Becker places this characteristic in the second half of the eighteenth century. See Carl L. Becker, *The Heavenly City of the Eighteenth Century Philosophers* (New Haven: Yale University Press, 1932), pp. 84-85.

CHAPTER VI

1. N. A. Popov, "Uchenye i literaturnye trudy V. N. Tatishcheva," *Torzhestvennoe sobranie Imperatorskoi Akademii Nauk*, IV (1887), 18.

2. Pekarskii, *op. cit.*, p. 31. Parts of Biron's accusations are quoted.

3. *Ibid.*, pp. 37-39, Tatishchev to Cherkasov, letter of 21 January 1742.

4. Tatishchev, "Razgovor." The Russian word *"nauka"* is commonly translated into English as "science." However, the word "knowledge" seems to suit better Tatishchev's use of it in the "Conversation."

5. Ivan Bolotnikov led a peasant revolt in 1607, and Stepan Razin led another in 1670.

6. See Chapter V.

7. The *Russkaia Pravda* was a collection of laws compiled in the first half of the eleventh century. The Soviet scholar A. I. Andreev claimed that the first evidence that Tatishchev possessed the *Pravda* was in 1737-1738. This reference in the "Conversation" would indicate that he found the *Pravda* sometime before 1733. A. I. Andreev, "Primechaniia V. N. Tatishcheva k 'Drevnim russkim zakonam,'" *Istoricheskie zapiski*, XXXVI (1951), 254-255.

8. The *Sudebnik* was the first law code of Muscovy. In the "Conversation," Tatishchev referred to the *Sudebnik* of 1564, which is probably a misprint. In his introduction to the Bartenev manuscript edition, he dated the *Sudebnik* at 1546. Later, in the 1740's, when he found a complete manuscript of the *Sudebnik*, he dated it correctly at 1550. Both editions are in Tatishchev, *Istoriia rossiiskaia v semi tomakh*, VII, 203-210 and 287-394.

9. On the Russian nobleman as *Kulturträger*, see Raeff, *Russian Intelligentsia*,

CHAPTER VII

1. N. I. Pavlenko, ed., "Materialy o razvitii ural'skoi promyshlennosti v 20-40kh godakh XVIIIv," *Istoricheskii arkhiv*, IX (1955), 159-161. For a summary of the growth of the Urals metal industry, see Pavlenko, *Istoriia metallurgii;* and V. I. Bezobrazov, "Vasilii Nikitich Tatishchev: Ocherk ego diatel'nost po gornoi chasti," *Torzhestvennoe sobranie Imperatorskoi Akademii Nauk*, IV (1887), 65-101.

2. Production statistics are available in Pavlenko, "Materialy o razvitii," pp. 170 and 176ff.

3. *PSZ*, IX, 290-296, No. 6559 for 23 March 1734. Pavlenko claimed that Tatishchev helped draft his "Instruction." See his editorial note in V. N. Tatishchev, "Nakaz Shikhtmeisteru [Sicktmeister] V. N. Tatishcheva," edited by N. I. Pavlenko, *Istoricheskii arkhiv*, VI (1951), 200.

4. V. N. Berkh, "Zhizneopisanie tainago sovetnika Vasiliia Nikiticha Tatishcheva," *Gornyi zhurnal*, I (1828), 109; and Popov, *Tatishchev*, pp. 143ff.

5. Pekarskii, *op. cit.*, pp. 32-34, Tatishchev to Biron, letter of 6 December 1734.

6. Berkh, *op. cit.*, pp. 109-111.

7. Popov outlined the Factory Statute in his biography: Popov, *Tatishchev*, pp. 544-549, n. 185. The Mining Statute is summarized in the introduction to M. A. Gorlovskii and N. I. Pavlenko, eds., "Materialy soveshaniia ural'skikh promyshlennikof 1734-1736gg," *Istoricheskii arkhiv*, IX (1955), 6-7.

8. Tatishchev, "Nakaz," pp. 210-288.

9. *Ibid.*, pp. 205-206.

10. Portal, *op. cit.*, pp. 94-96.

11. V. N. Tatishchev, "Instruktsiia V. N. Tatishcheva o poriadke prepodovaniia v shkolakh pri ural'skikh kazennykh zavodakh," edited by N. F. Demidova, *Istoricheskie arkhiv*, V (1950), 166-178.

12. For the history of Russian education until 1734, see Patrick L. Alston, *Education and the State in Tsarist Russia* (Stanford: Stanford University Press, 1969), pp. 3-9; and William H. Johnson, *Russia's Educational Heritage* (New York: Octagon Books, 1969), pp. 3-42.

13. Grau, *op. cit.*, p. 69.

14. A. I. Andreev, "Trudy V. N. Tatishcheva po geografii Rossii" in V. N. Tatishchev, *Izbrannye trudy po geografii Rossii*, edited by A. I. Andreev (Moscow: Gosudarstvennoe Izdatel'stvo Geograficheskoi Literatury, 1950), pp. 14-16; and E. G. Shapot, "Ankety V. N. Tatishcheva kak istochnik po istorii Sibiri pervoi poloviny XVIIIv," *Problemy istochnikovedeniia*, X (1962), 137-138.

15. V. N. Tatishchev, "Obshchee geograficheskoi opisanie vseia Siberi" in his *Izbrannye trudy*, pp. 43-76.

16. Andreev, "Trudy V. N. Tatishcheva," pp. 12-13; and Shapot, *op. cit.*, pp. 139-153.

17. V. N. Tatishchev, "Predlozhenie o sochinenii istorii i geografii rossiiskoi" in his *Izbrannye trudy*, pp. 77-106.

18. Only three volumes of the *Lexicon* have been published. Tatishchev, *Leksikon rossiskoi.*

19. Some of these letters have been published in Grau, *op. cit.*, Appendix, pp. 209-215.

20. *Ibid.*, pp. 213-215.

21. V. N. Tatishchev, "Proshenie ural'skikh promyshlennikov imperitsa Anne Ivanovne po povodu vvedeniia Tatishchevym instituta shikhtmeisterov," edited by N. I. Pavlenko, *Istoricheskii arkhiv*, VI (1951), 208-231.

22. V. N. Tatishchev, "Rezoliutsiia kantseliarii glavnogo pravleniia sibirskikh i kazenskikh zavodov po povodu prosheniia zavodchikov," edited by N. I. Pavlenko, *Istoricheskii arkhiv*, VI (1951), 231-235.

23. V. N. Tatishchev, "Razsuzhdenie Komerts-Kollegii Kabinetu ministrov 'O nakaze shikhtmeisteru,'" edited by N. I. Pavlenko, *Istorischeskii arkhiv*, VI (1951), 235-240.

24. Kafengauz, *Istoriia*, pp. 174-175. See also Popov, *Tatishchev*, pp. 150-151; and Berkh, *op. cit.*, pp. 116-118. Demidov bribed Biron at a cost of 50,000 rubles.

110

25. Bestuzhev-Riumin, *op. cit.*, p. 33.

26. Portal, *op. cit.*, p. 97.

CHAPTER VIII

1. Boris Nolde, *La Formation de l'Empire Russe* (Paris: Institut d'Etudes Slaves de l'Université de Paris, 1952), pp. 191-217. The Bashkirs were a Turcic speaking people. The Kalmyks migrated into the Ural Mountains in the Seventeenth century. They were Buddhists and spoke a Mongol tongue. The Kazakhs, a Muslim and Turcic speaking people, were divided into three realms: the Junior, Middle, and Senior Hundreds. The Junior and Middle Hundreds inhabited the South Urals region. See also Alton S. Donnelly, *The Russian Conquest of Bashkiria, 1552-1740: A Case Study in Imperialism* (New Haven: Yale University Press, 1968); and George V. Lantzeff, *Siberia in the Seventeenth Century* (Berkeley: University of California Press, 1943).

2. M. G. Novlianskaia, "Nauchnye raboty Orenburgskoi ekspeditsii (1734-1737gg)," *Trudy Instituta istorii estestvoznaniia i tekhniki*, XXVII (1959), 26-43. See also M. G. Novlianskaia, *Ivan Kirilovich Kirilov* (Leningrad-Moscow: Izdatel'stvo "Nauk," 1964), pp. 86-133.

3. On this point, see Nolde, *op. cit.*, pp. 218-224.

4. The troops were to be used in the Russian-Turkish War of 1735-1739.

5. Solov'ev, *Istoriia Rossii*, Book X, Vol. 20, pp. 591-593.

6. Parts of letter quoted *ibid.*, p. 599.

7. *Ibid.*, pp. 599-600.

8. Donnelly, *op. cit.*, pp. 97-98; and Berkh, *op. cit.*, pp. 120-121.

9. Tatishchev summarized the discussion in a letter to Soimonov in December 1737. The letter was published in Solov'ev, *Istoriia Rossii*, Book X, Vol. 20, pp. 600-601.

10. In 1743, the location of Orenburg was moved again approximately 30 miles west to the juncture of the Sakmara and Ural Rivers.

11. Donnelly, *op. cit.*, pp. 102-105.

12. *Ibid.*, pp. 106-109.

13. *Ibid.*, pp. 109-116; see also Tatishchev's letter to Empress Anne of 9 May 1738, published in Solov'ev, *Istoriia Rossii*, Book X, Vol. 20, pp. 604-605.

14. Lantzeff, *op. cit.*, p. 93.

15. Solov'ev, *Istoriia Rossii*, Book X, Vol. 20, p. 605.

16. Donnelly, *op. cit.*, p. 118.

17. Andreev, "Trudy V. N. Tatishcheva," pp. 11-12.

18. V. N. Tatishchev, "Predstavleniia polkovnika Zmeeva i postanovleniia Tatishcheva i Soimonova, o poselenii kalmyskoi kniagini Anny Taishinoi v Stovropol'skoi Kreposti na Volge." Document published in Popov, *Tatishchev*, Appendix, pp. 620-630. See Chapter X.

19. Solov'ev, *Istoriia Rossii*, Book X, Vol. 20, p. 606.

20. *Ibid.*, p. 607.

21. Nolde, *op. cit.*, p. 225. Nolde apparently was not aware that Tatishchev proposed the use of the Bashkirs in Russian service as well as having formed the contingent.

CHAPTER IX

1. Tatishchev, *Dukhovanaiia*. An incomplete and somewhat inaccurate translation of the *Testament* was made in the nineteenth century: *The Testament of Basil Tatishchev*, translated by John Martinof (Paris: Benjamin Duprat, 1860).

2. Andreev, "Trudy V. N. Tatishcheva," pp. 14-16.

3. A. I. Andreev, "Donoshenie V. N. Tatishcheva v pravitel'stvuiushchii senat po voprosom organizatsii Kartograficheskikh rabot 30 aprelia 1739g" in Tatishchev, *Izbrannye trudy*, pp. 98-106.

4. Tatishchev, *Leksikon rossiskoi.*

5. Andreev, "Trudy V. N. Tatishcheva," p. 17.

6. V. N. Tatishchev, "Russia ili kak nyne zovut Rossia," in his *Izbrannye trudy*, pp. 107-142. "Russia" was the former name of the Russian land. The apparent discrepancy is due to transliteration.

7. The origin of the name "Rus" is still a controversial matter. Vernadsky believes that the name derived from the river Ros. See George Vernadsky, *The Origins of Russia* (Oxford: Clarendon Press, 1959), p. 212. For a lengthy discussion on the topic, see Henryk Paszkiewicz, *The Making of the Russian Nation* (Great Britain: Henry Regnery Company, 1963), pp. 110-175. Paszkiewicz says that he does not reject the idea that the word "Rus" was derived from the "reddish" color of those people (pp. 119-120). He did not refer to Tatishchev on the topic.

8. A guberniia was the largest territorial division in Imperial Russia. Tatishchev's inclusion of Moscow in his Belorusskaia Guberniia seems misplaced, since the traditional area for Belorussia is farther west. In the document, he placed the Moscow district in the list for Velikorusskaia Guberniia, even though it is numbered according to the listing for Belorusskaia Guberniia. The only solution to this apparent inconsistency would be to examine the original manuscript.

9. The letter is printed in Solov'ev, *Istoriia Rossii*, Book X, Vol. 20, pp. 658-659.

10. Popov, *Tatishchev*, pp. 200-205.

11. D. A. Korsakov, *Iz zhizni russkikh deiatelei XVIII veka* (Kazan: Imperatorskii Kazanskii Universitet, 1891), pp. 283-330.

12. Rogger, *op. cit.*, pp. 26-27.

13. Grau, *op. cit.*, p. 96.

14. Korsakov, *Iz zhizni*, pp. 283-307.

15. The members of the circle must have changed from time to time. By the mid-1730's, Prince Kantemir was in France; and Soimonov, Khrushchev, and Urusov, not to mention Tatishchev, were in the Urals region.

112

16. Iu. Got'e, " 'Proekt o popravlenii gosudarstvennykh del' Artemii Petrovichs Volynskogo," *Delo i dni*, III (1922), 1-31. Got'e attempted to reconstruct the General Project from the fragments. He quoted extensively from the document.

17. Grau, *op. cit.*, p. 96.

18. Tatishchev, *Dukhovanaia.*

19. See Chapter VI.

20. Tatishchev obviously meant the "Generality," or upper nobility.

21. Andreev, "Trudy V. N. Tatishcheva," p. 20.

CHAPTER X

1. Popov, *Tatishchev*, pp. 264ff.

2. For background, see *Ibid.*, p. 335ff.

3. N. N. Palmov, "K astrakhanskomu periodu zhizni V. N. Tatishcheva," *Izvestiia rossiiskoi akademii nauk*, Series VI, Vol. 19 (1925), pp. 202-204.

4. Popov, *Tatishchev*, pp. 274ff.

5. Palmov, *op. cit.*, pp. 204-206.

6. V. N. Tatishchev, "Ovybnykh lovliakh," document published in Palmov, *op. cit.*, pp. 206-210.

7. V. N. Tatishchev, "Postanovlenie Tatishcheva s tovarishchami o rybnykh lovliakh dlia Kalmykhov okolo Astrakhani" in Popov, *Tatishchev*, Appendix VII, pp. 635-640.

8. Tatishchev did not specifically explain what he meant by *"obrok."* In all probability, he inferred that the Kalmyks would have to turn a certain percentage of their catches over to the State.

9. Empress Anne died in October 1740. She appointed the infant Prince of Brunswick as Emperor Ivan VI, with Biron as Regent. The following November, Anne of Mecklenburg assumed the throne in a palace revolution. Biron was exiled to Siberia. In November 1741, however, the Preobrazhenskii regiment carried out yet another palace revolution and proclaimed Elizabeth Empress. Ostermann, Münnich, and Count M. G. Golovkin were exiled to Siberia.

10. Popov, *Tatishchev*, pp. 247ff.

11. *Ibid.*, pp. 355-364. See also Jonas Hanway, *An Historical Account of the British Trade over the Caspian Sea: With a Journal of Travels from London through Russia into Persia; and Back Again through Russia, Germany, and Holland*, I (London: 1753), 122ff.

12. Pekarskii, *op. cit.*, pp. 29-30, Tatishchev to Cherkasov, letter of 27 February 1742.

13. *Ibid.*, p. 40. Tatishchev to Cherkasov, letter of 2 January 1743.

14. Popov, *Tatishchev*, pp. 373-375.

15. V. N. Tatishchev, "Na pamiat' o delakh astrakhanskikh," edited by P. I. Alefirenko, *Istoricheskii arkhiv*, VII (1951), 403-407.

16. V. N. Tatishchev, "Predlozhenie o razmnozhenii fabriku," edited by N. I. Pavlenko, *Istoricheskii arkhiv*, VII (1951), 407-410.

17. Popov, *Tatishchev*, pp. 368 and 375-385.

18. Hanway, *op. cit.*, I, 13-15 and 82.

19. *Ibid.*, II, 13 and 37-39.

20. *Ibid.*, pp. 74-75.

21. *Ibid.*, I, 117-122.

22. *Ibid.*, p. 117.

23. In all probability, this granddaughter was the daughter of his son Evgraf, who lived with Tatishchev at that time.

24. Hanway, *op. cit.*, I, 128.

25. *Ibid.*, p. 119.

26. Tatishchev referred to these maps in his "O geografii voobshche i o russkoi," in *Izbrannye trudy*, p. 217.

27. V. N. Tatishchev, "Vvedenie k gistoricheskomu i geograficheskomu opisanii Velokorusskiiskoi Imperia," *ibid.*, pp. 143-197.

28. Tatishchev, *Leksikon rossiskoi*.

29. Pekarskii, *op. cit.*, p. 43, Tatishchev to Cherkasov, letter of 30 October 1744. See also Tatishchev's letter of 31 December 1743 to I. I. Nepliuev, Governor of Orenburg, in Palmov, *op. cit.*, p. 208.

30. V. N. Tatishchev, "Napomnenie na prislannoe rospisanie vysokikh i nizhnikh gosudarstvennykh i semskikh pravitel'stv" in his *Izbrannye trudy*, pp. 198-206. Andreev noted that the "Napomnenie" was found with notes to another manuscript, "Rospis' pravitel'stv rossiiskikh," in which Tatishchev proposed a territorial division of the Empire. Tatishchev was probably referring to this "Rospis'" in the title of the "Napomnenie." Although the "Napomnenie" was not considered by the Senate, it was brought to Empress Elizabeth's attention in 1746; see p. 207, n. 1.

31. Solov'ev, *Istoriia Rossii*, Book XI, Vol. 22, pp. 331-334.

32. Pekarskii, *op. cit.*, pp. 45-46, Tatishchev to Cherkasov, letter of 27 December 1745.

CHAPTER XI

1. V. N. Tatishchev, "Naprimer predstavienie o kupechestve i remeslakh," edited by P. I. Alefirenko, *Istoricheskii arkhiv*, VII (1951), 410-426. See also Tatishchev's letter to Vorontsov of 12 May 1748 in Tatishchev, "Perepiska," pp. 279-281.

2. On this basis, Alefirenko and I. S. Bak have argued that Tatishchev cannot be considered as a mercantilist in the classical sense of the term. See P. I. Alefirenko, "Ekonomicheskie vzgliady V. N. Tatishcheva," *Voprosy istorii*, XII (1948), 89-96; and I. S. Bak, "Ekonomicheskie vozzreniia V. N. Tatishcheva," *Istoricheskie zapiski*, LIV (1958), 362-381.

3. Tatishchev, *Leksikon rossiskoi*. Only the first three parts (up to the letter "K") were published.

4. V. N. Tatishchev, "Napomnenie na prislannoe opisanie narodov, chto v opisanii geograficheskom nablindat' nuzhdno" in his *Izbrannye trudy*, pp. 229-235.

5. A. A. Shakhmatov, "K voprosu o kriticheskom izdanii 'Istorii rossiiskoi' V. N. Tatishcheva," *Dela i dni*, I (1920), 82.

6. Rogger, *op. cit.*, pp. 190-197.

7. Tatishchev's letter of 30 September 1746 to Razumovskii, Tatishchev, "Perepiska," pp. 255-256.

8. Letter published in Hanway, *op. cit.*, I, 118-119.

9. *Ibid.*, p. 118.

10. *Ibid.*, p. 119.

11. After Tatishchev's death, Gerhard Müller edited and published the *Russian History: Istoriia rossiiskaia s samykh drevneishikh vremen neusypnymi trudami cherez tritsat' let sobrannaia i opisannaia pokoinym tainym sovetnikom i astrakhanskim gubernatorom, Vasil'em Nikitichem Tatishchem*, edited by Gerhard Friedrich Müller (5 vols.; Moscow: 1768, 1769, 1773, 1774, and 1784). The historian M. P. Pogodin found another manuscript of the fourth part in 1845, and the Imperial Historical Society published it in 1848. Soviet scholars have published a new edition which contains background notes and appendices of manuscript variations: *Istoriia rossiiskaia v semi tomakh*, edited by A. I. Andreev, S. N. Valk, and M. N. Tikhomirov (7 vols.; Leningrad-Moscow: Izdatel'stvo Akademii Nauk SSSR and Izdatel'stvo "Nauk," 1962, 1963, 1964, 1965, 1966, and 1968).

12. Tatishchev, *Istoriia rossiiskaia v semi tomakh*, I (1962), 90.

13. *Ibid.*, pp. 79ff.

14. See Chapter V.

15. V. N. Tatishchev, "O geografii voobshche i o russkoi," "Drevnee razdelenie Russii," and "O drevnem pravitel'stve ruskom i drugikh v primer" in his *Istoriia rossiiskaia v semi tomakh*, I (1962), 345-370.

16. For Tatishchev and the Norman Theory, see Chapter III.

17. Anatole G. Mazour, *Modern Russian Historiography* (Princeton: D. van Nostrand Co., Inc., 1958), p. 11.

18. Rogger, *op. cit.*, p. 198.

19. Tatishchev, *Istoriia rossiiskaia v semi tomakh*, I (1962), 372; II (1963), 33; and IV (1964), 112-113. See also V. M. Morgailo, "Rabota V. N. Tatishcheva nad tekstom Ioakimovskoi Letopisi," *Arkheograficheskii ezhegodnik za 1962 god*, 1963, pp. 260-268.

20. N. M. Karamzin, *Istoriia gosudarstva Russkogo*, VII (St. Petersburg: 1835), 271-272.

21. S. L. Peshtich, *Russkaia istoriografiia XVIII veka*, I (Leningrad: Izdatel' stvo Leningradskogo Universiteta, 1961), 222ff.

22. M. N. Tikhomirov, "O russkikh istochnik Istorie rossiiskoi" in Tatishchev, *Istoriia rossiiskaia v semi tomakh*, I (1962), pp. 40-53.

23. H. C. Schlieper, "Tatishchev's Interest in History," *New Review*, V (1965), 17-24; quote on p. 18. It should be noted that Schlieper's article contains several factual errors in the biographical information.

24. On this point, see Cassirer, *op. cit.*, pp. 203-208.

25. Rogger, *op. cit.*, pp. 201-202.

26. A. Dmitriev, "Predsmertnoe uveshchanie V. N. Tatishcheva synu," *Zhurnal ministerstva narodnago prosveshcheniia*, CCXLIV (1886), 225-230.

27. *Ibid.*, pp. 231-237. Dmitriev noted that an unknown eyewitness wrote down Tatishchev's last words.

28. *Ibid.*, p. 237.

Bibliography

I. PRINCIPAL WRITINGS OF V. N. TATISHCHEV

BOOKS

Dukhovanaiia tainago sovetnika, i astrakhanskago gubernatora Vasiliia Nikiticha Tatishcheva. St. Petersburg: 1773.

Istoriia rossiiskaia s samykh drevneishikh vremen neusypnymi trudami cherez tritsat' let sobrannaia i opisannaia pokoinym tainym sovetnikom i astrakhanskim gubernatorom, Vasil'em Nikitichem Tatishchem. Edited by Gerhard Friedrich Müller. 5 vols. Moscow: 1768, 1769, 1773, 1774, 1784, and 1848.

Istoriia rossiiskaia v semi tomakh. Edited by A. I. Andreev, S. N. Valk, and M. N. Tikhomirov. 7 vols. Leningrad-Moscow: Izdatel'stvo Akademii Nauk SSSR and Izdatel'stvo "Nauk," 1962, 1963, 1964, 1965, 1966, and 1968.

Izbrannye trudy po geografii Rossii. Edited by A. I. Andreev. Moscow: Gosudarstvennoe Izdatel'stvo Geograficheskoi Literatury, 1950.

Leksikon rossiskoi, istoricheskoi, geograficheskoi, politicheskoi, i grazhdanskoi, sochinennyi gospodinom tainym sovetnikom i astrakhanskim gubernatorum Vasil'em Nikitichem Tatishchevym. 3 vols. St. Petersburg: Gornyi Ulchilishch, 1793.

The Testament of Basil Tatishchev. Translated by John Martinof. Paris: Benjamin Duprat, 1860.

ARTICLES

In *Chteniia v imperatorskom obshchestve istorii i drevnostei rossiskikh pri moskovskom universitete:*

"Razgovor dvukh priatelei o pol'ze nauk i uchilishch." Edited by N. A. Popov. I (1887), 1-171.

In *Istoricheskii arkhiv:*

"Ekonomicheskie zapiski V. N. Tatishcheva." Edited by P. I. Alefirenko. VII (1951), 397-402.

"Instruktsiia V. N. Tatishcheva o poriadke prepodovaniia v shkolakh pri ural'skikh kazennykh zavodakh." Edited by N. F. Demidova. V (1950), 166-178.

"Nakaz Shikhtmeisteru [sicktmeister] V. N. Tatishcheva." Edited by N. I. Pavlenko. VI (1951), 199-207.

117

"Na pamiat' o delakh astrakhanskikh." Edited by P. I. Alefirenko. VII (1951), 403-407.

"Naprimer predstavienie o kupechestve i remeslakh." Edited by P. I. Alefirenko. VII (1951), 410-426.

"Perepiska V. N. Tatishcheva za 1746-1750 gg." Edited by A. I. Andreev. VI (1951), 245-314.

"Predlozhenie o razmnozhenii fabriku." Edited by N. I. Pavlenko. VII (1951), 407-410.

"Proshenie ural'skikh promyshlennikov imperitsa Anne Ivanovne po povodu vvedeniia Tatishchevym instituta shikhtmeisterov." Edited by N. I. Pavlenko. VI (1951), 208-231.

"Razsuzhdenie Komerts-Kollegii Kabinetu ministrov 'O nakaze shikhtmeisteru.' " Edited by N. I. Pavlenko. VI (1951), 235-240.

"Rezoliutsiia kantseliarii glavnogo pravleniia sibirskikh i kazenskikh zavodov po povodu prosheniia zavodchikov." Edited by N. I. Pavlenko. VI (1951), 231-235.

In *Utro:*

"Proizvol'noe i soglasnoe razsuzhdenie i mnenie sobravshagosia shliakhtstva russkago o pravlenii gosudarstvennom." Edited by M. P. Pogodin. 1859, 369-379.

II. PUBLIC DOCUMENT

Russia. *Polnoe sobranie zakonov Rossiiskoi Imperii s 1649 goda* [PSZ]. VI, VII, IX. St. Petersburg: 1830.

III. BOOKS

Alston, Patrick L. *Education and the State in Tsarist Russia.* Stanford: Stanford University Press, 1969.

Anderson, Thornton. *Russian Political Thought.* Ithaca, N. Y.: Cornell University Press, 1967.

Becker, Carl L. *The Heavenly City of the Eighteenth Century Philosophers.* New Haven: Yale University Press, 1932.

Berkov, P. I. *Istoriia russkoi zhurnalistiki XVIII veka.* Moscow: 1952.

————. *Problemy russkogo prosveshcheniia v literature XVIII veka.* Leningrad-Moscow: Izdatel'stvo Akademii Nauk SSSR, 1961.

Bestuzhev-Riumin, K. N. *Biografii i kharakteristiki.* St. Petersburg: V. S. Balashev, 1882.

Betiaev, Ia. *Sotsial'noe-politicheskaia i filosofskaia mysl' Rossii epokhi petrovskikh preobrazovanii.* Moscow: Izdatel'stvo Akademii Nauk SSSR, 1946.

118

Cassirer, Ernst. *The Philosophy of the Enlightenment.* Translated by Fritz Koelln and James Pettegrove. Princeton: Princeton University Press, 1951.

Chistovich, I. A. *Theofan Prokopovich i ego vremia.* St. Petersburg: Izdanie Imperatorskoi Akademii Nauk, 1868.

Confino, Michael. *Domaines et Seigneurs en Russie vers la Fin du XVIIIe Siècle: Etude de Structures Agraires et de Mentalités Economiques.* Paris: Institut d'Etudes Slaves de l'Université de Paris, 1963.

Cracraft, James. *The Church Reform of Peter the Great.* Stanford: Stanford University Press, 1971.

Deich, G. M. *V. N. Tatishchev.* Sverdlovsk: 1962.

Donnelly, Alton S. *The Russian Conquest of Bashkiria, 1552–1740: A Case Study in Imperialism.* New Haven: Yale University Press, 1968.

Feigina, S. A. *Alandskii kongress.* Moscow: Izdatel'stvo Akademii Nauk SSSR, 1959.

Florinsky, Michael T. *Russia: A History and an Interpretation.* Vol. I. New York: The Macmillan Company, 1953.

Gagliardo, John G. *Enlightened Despotism.* New York: Thomas Crowell Co., 1967.

Gay, Peter. *The Enlightenment: An Interpretation. The Rise of Modern Paganism.* New York: Vintage Books, 1966.

Golutsev, V. A. *Zakonodatel'stvo i pravo v Rossii XVIII veka.* St. Petersburg: 1896.

Grau, Conrad. *Der Wirtschaftsorganisator, Staatsmann und Wissenschaftler Vasilij N. Tatiščev.* Berlin: Akademie-Verlag, 1963.

Gukovskii, G. A. *Russkaia literatura XVIII veka.* Moscow: Gosudarstvennoe Uchebno-Pedagogicheskoi Izdatel'stvo, 1939.

Hans, Nicholas. *History of Russian Educational Policy.* New York: Russell & Russell, Inc., 1964.

Hanway, Jonas. *An Historical Account of the British Trade over the Caspian Sea: With a Journal of Travels from London through Russia into Persia; and Back Again through Russia, Germany, and Holland.* 2 vols. London: 1753.

Harrison, John A. *The Founding of the Russian Empire in Asia and America.* Coral Gables, Florida: University of Miami Press, 1971.

Hazard, Paul. *The European Mind.* Translated by J. Lewis May. Cleveland: The World Publishing Co., 1968.

————. *European Thought in the Eighteenth Century.* Translated by J. Lewis May. Cleveland: The World Publishing Co., 1969.

119

Iofa, L. E. *Sovremenniki Lomonosova I. K. Kirilov i V. N. Tatishchev.* Moscow: Izdatel'stvo Akademii Nauk SSSR, 1949.

Istoricheskii ocherk i obzor fondov rukopisnogo otdela biblioteki Akademii Nauk. Vol. II. Leningrad-Moscow: Izdatel'stvo Akademii Nauk SSSR, 1958.

Istoriia istoricheskoi nauki v SSSR. Bibliografiia. Moscow: Izdatel'stvo "Nauk," 1965.

Johnson, William H. *Russia's Educational Heritage.* New York: Octagon Books, 1969.

Kafengauz, B. B. *Istoriia khoziaistva Demidovykh v XVIII-XIXvv.* Vol. I. Leningrad-Moscow: Izdatel'stvo Akademii Nauk SSSR, 1949.

Kantemir, A. D. *Sobranie stikhotvorenii.* Leningrad: Sovetskii Pisatel', 1956.

Karamzin, N. M. *Istoriia gosudarstva Russkogo.* Vol. VII. St. Petersburg: 1835.

Kliuchevskii, V. O. *Kurs ruskoi istorii.* Vol. IV. Moscow: Gosudarstvennoe Sotsial'no-Ekonomicheskoe Izdatel'stvo, 1937.

Koblens, I. N. *Andrei Ivanovich Bogdanov.* Moscow: Izdatel'stvo Akademii Nauk SSSR, 1958.

Kolarz, Walter. *Russia and Her Colonies.* New York: Frederick A. Praeger Co., Inc., 1952.

Korsakov, D. A. *Iz zhizni russkikh deiatelei XVIII veka.* Kazan: Imperatorskii Kazanskii Universitet, 1891.

————. *Votsarenie imperatritsy Anny Ioannovny.* Kazan: Imperatorskii Kazanskii Universitet, 1880.

Lantzeff, George V. *Siberia in the Seventeenth Century.* Berkeley: University of California Press, 1943.

Manstein, Christoff von. *Memoirs of Russia.* London: Becket and De Hondt, 1770.

Mazour, Anatole G. *Modern Russian Historiography.* Princeton: D. van Nostrand Co., Inc., 1958.

Miliukov, Pavel. *Gosudarstvennoe khoziastvo Rossii v pervoi chetverti XVIII stoletiia i reforma Petra Velikago.* St. Petersburg: V. S. Balashev, 1892.

————. *Iz istorii russkoi intelligentsii.* St. Petersburg: Tipografiia Montvid, 1903.

Montesquieu, Charles Louis de Secondat. *L'Esprit des Lois.* Books III, VIII, XV, and XVIII. Paris: Garnier Frères, n.d.

Nolde, Boris. *La Formation de l'Empire Russe.* Paris: Institut d'Etudes Slaves de l'Université de Paris, 1952.

Novlianskaia, M. G. *Ivan Kirilovich Kirilov.* Leningrad-Moscow: Izdatel'stvo "Nauk," 1964.

Oliva, L. Jay. *Russia in the Era of Peter the Great.* Englewood Cliffs, N. J.: Prentice-Hall, Inc., 1969.

Paszkiewicz, Henryk. *The Making of the Russian Nation.* Great Britain: Henry Regnery Company, 1963.

Pavlenko, N. I. *Istoriia metallurgii v Rossii XVIII veka.* Moscow: Izdatel'stvo Akademii Nauk SSSR, 1962.

—————. *Razvitie metallurgicheskoi promyshlennosti Rossii v pervoi polovine XVIIIv.* Moscow: Izdatel'stvo Akademii Nauk SSSR, 1953.

Peshtich, S. L. *Russkaia istoriografiia XVIII veka.* Vol. I. Leningrad: Izdatel'stvo Leningradskogo Universiteta, 1961.

Plekhanov, G. V. *History of Russian Social Thought.* New York: P. W. A. Project of U. S. Government, 1938.

—————. *Istoriia ruskoi obshchestvennoi mysli.* Vol. II. Moscow: Tvorchestvo "Mir," 1918.

Popov, N. A. *Uchenye i literaturnye trudy V. N. Tatishcheva.* St. Petersburg: Imperatorskaia Akademia Nauk, 1887.

—————. *V. N. Tatishchev i ego vremia.* Moscow: Soldatenkov i Shchepkin, 1861.

Portal, Roger. *L'Oural au XVIIIᵉ Siècle: Etude d'Histoire Economique et Sociale.* Paris: Institut d'Etudes Slaves de l'Université de Paris, 1950.

Radovskii, M. I. *Antiokh Kantemir i peterburskaia Akademiia Nauk.* Leningrad-Moscow: Izdatel'stvo Akademii Nauk SSSR, 1959.

Raeff, Marc. *Imperial Russia 1682–1825: The Coming of Age of Modern Russia.* New York: Alfred A. Knopf, Inc., 1971.

—————. *Origins of the Russian Intelligentsia.* New York: Harcourt, Brace & World, Inc., 1966.

—————, ed. *Plans for Political Reform in Imperial Russia, 1730–1905.* Englewood Cliffs, N. J.: Prentice-Hall, Inc., 1966.

—————, ed. *Russian Intellectual History: An Anthology.* New York: Harcourt, Brace & World, Inc., 1966.

Rogger, Hans. *National Consciousness in Eighteenth Century Russia.* Cambridge: Harvard University Press, 1960.

Shcherbatov, M. M. *On the Corruption of Morals in Russia.* Edited and translated by Antony Lentin. Cambridge: Cambridge University Press, 1969.

Senigov, I. *Istoriko-kriticheskoi issledovanie o novgorodskikh letopisiakh i o Rossiiskoi istorii V. N. Tatishchev.* Moscow: "Chtenia" Imperatorskago Obshchestva Istorii i Drevnostei, 1887.

Shackleton, Robert. *Montesquieu: A Critical Biography*. Oxford: Oxford University Press, 1961.

Shaskol'skii, I. P. *Normanskaia teoria v sovremennoi burzhuaznoi nauke*. Leningrad. Izdatel'stvo "Nauk," 1965.

Solov'ev, S. M. *Istoriia Rossii s drevneishikh vremen*. Books IX, X, and XI. Moscow: Izdatel'stvo Sotsial'no-Ekonomicheskoi Literatury, 1962–1964.

Sukhomlinov, M. I. *Istoriia rossiiskoi Akademii*. Vol. V. St. Petersburg: Imperatorskaia Akademia Nauk, 1880.

Tatishchev, S. S. *Rod Tatishchevykh 1400–1900*. St. Petersburg: 1900.

Theofan [Prokopovich], Archbishop of Novgorod. *Sochineniia*. Leningrad-Moscow: Izdatel'stvo Akademii Nauk SSSR, 1961.

Utechin, S. V. *Russian Political Thought*. New York: Frederick A. Praeger Co., Inc., 1963.

Vernadsky, George. *The Origins of Russia*. Oxford: Clarendon Press, 1959.

Winter, Eduard. *Halle als Ausgangspunkt der Deutschen Russlandkunde in 18. Jahrhundert*. Berlin: Adademie-Verlag, 1953.

Wittram, Reinhard. *Peter I: Czar und Kaiser*. 2 vols. Göttingen: Vandenhoeck & Ruprecht, 1964.

IV. ARTICLES

Alefirenko, P. I. "Ekonomicheskie vzgliady V. N. Tatishcheva." *Voprosy istorii*, XII (1948), 89-96.

―――――. "Sotsial'no-politicheskie vozzreniia V. N. Tatishcheva." *Voprosy istorii*, X (1951), 103-116.

Aleksandrov, S. A. "Ekonomicheskie i politicheskie vzgliady V. N. Tatishcheva." *Izvestiia Akademii Nauk SSSR (Otdelenie ekonomiki i prava)*, III (1951), 186-207.

Andreev, A. I. "Primechaniia V. N. Tatishcheva k 'Drevnim russkim zakonam.'" *Istoricheskie zapiski*, XXXVI (1951), 252-262.

Bak, I. S. "Ekonomicheskie vozzreniia V. N. Tatishcheva." *Istoricheskie zapiski*, LIV (1958), 362-381.

Berkh, V. N. "Zhizneopisanie tainago sovetnika Vasiliia Nikiticha Tatishcheva." *Gornyi zhurnal*, I (1828), 109-121.

Bezobrazov, V. I. "Vasilii Nikitich Tatishchev: Ocherk ego diatel'nost po gornoi chasti." *Torzhestvennoe sobranie Imperatorskoi Akademii Nauk*, IV (1887), 65-101.

Bialeskii, K. A. "Metallurgicheskaia laboratoriia berg-kollegii." *Trudy instituta esvoznaniia i tekhniki*, III (1953), 176-183.

122

Blanc, Simone. "La Pratique de l'Administration Russe dans la Première Moitié du XVIIIᵉ Siècle." *Revue d'Histoire Moderne et Contemporaine,* X (1963), 45-64.

————. "Tatiscev et la pratique du mercantilisme." *La Russie et l'Europe.* (1970), 169-184.

Dmitriev, A. "Predsmertnoe uveshchanie V. N. Tatishcheva synu." *Zhurnal ministerstva narodnago prosveshcheniia,* CCXLIV (1886), 225-237.

Epifanov, P. P. " 'Uchenaia druzhina' i prosvetitel'stvo XVIII veka." *Voprosy istorii,* III (March 1963), 37-53.

Geiermans, G. L. "Tatishchevskie spiski 'Russkoi pravdy.' " *Problemy istochnikovedeniia,* III (1940), 164ff.

"Geschichte der Familie der Grossfürstin und Regentin Anna und der Herzogs Anton Ulrich von Braunschweig." *Büschings Magazin,* XXII (1788), 495.

Gorlovskii, M. A. "K istorii osnovaniia Ekaterinburga." *Istoricheskie zapiski,* XXXIX (1952), 159-180.

————, and Pavlenko, N. I., eds. "Materialy soveshaniia ural'skikh promyshlennikof 1734-1736gg." *Istoricheskii arkhiv,* IX (1955), 6-7.

Got'e, Iu. " 'Proekt o popravlenii gosudarstvennykh del' Artemii Petrovichs Volynskogo." *Delo i dni,* III (1922), 1-31.

Gurvich, D. M. "V. N. Tatishchev i russkaia arkheologicheskaia nauka." *Sovetskaia arkheologiia,* XXVI (1956), 153-164.

Ivanov, A. I. "V. N. Tatishchev kak issledovatel' karstovykh iavlenii." *Voprosy istorii estestvoznaniia i tekhniki,* IV (1957), 86-93.

Kafengauz, B. B. "Stroitel'stvo pervykh ural'skikh zavodov." *Voprosy istorii,* V-VI (1945), 50ff.

Kaplan, Frederick I. "Tatishchev and Kantemir, Two Eighteenth Century Exponents of a Russian Bureaucratic Style of Thought." *Jahrbücher fur Geschichte Osteuropas,* XIII (1965), 497-510.

Kolosov, E. E. "Novye biograficheskie materialy o V. N. Tatishcheve." *Arkheograficheskii ezhegodnik za 1963 god,* 1964, pp. 107-113.

Korsakov, D. A. "Artemii Petrovich Volynnskoi i ego 'konfidenty.' " *Russkaia starina,* XLVIII, 17-54.

Koutaissoff, E. "Tatishchev's Joachim Chronicle." *University of Birmingham Historical Journal,* III, No. 1, pp. 52-63.

Kuz'min, A. G. "Ob istochnikovedcheskoi osnove 'Istorii rossiiskoi' V. N. Tatishcheva." *Voprosy istorii,* IX (Sept. 1963), 214-218.

Morgailo, V. M. "Rabota V. N. Tatishcheva nad tekstom Ioakimovskoi Letopisi." *Arkheograficheskii ezhegodnik za 1962 god,* 1963, pp. 260-268.

123

Novlianskaia, M. G. "Nauchnye raboty Orenburgskoi ekspeditsii (1734–1737gg)." *Trudy Instituta istorii estestvoznaniia i tekhniki,* XXVII (1959), 26-43.

Palmov, N. N. "K astrakhanskomu periodu zhizni V. N. Tatishcheva." *Izvestiia rossiiskoi akademii nauk,* Series VI, Vol. XIX (1925), pp. 202ff.

Pankratov, V. P. "Filosofiskie i sotsial'no-politicheskie vozzrenniia V. N. Tatishcheva." *Vestnik moskovskoi universiteta,* VIII (1947), 131-134.

Pavlenko, N. I., ed. "Materialy o razvitii ural'skoi promyshlennosti v 20-40kh godakh XVIIIv." *Istoricheskii arkhiv,* IX (1955), 156-282.

Pekarskii, P. P. "Novyia izvestiia o V. N. Tatishcheve." *Zapiski Imperatorskoi Akademii Nauk,* IV (1864), 8-46.

Pogodin, M. N. "Otkrytiia dlia russkoi istorii." *Moskvitianin,* VII (1843), 229-231.

Popov, N. A. "Uchenye i literaturnye trudy V. N. Tatishcheva." *Torzhestvennoe sobranie Imperatorskoi Akademii Nauk,* IV (1887), 1-64.

Protasov, G. A. "Zapiska Tatishcheva o 'Proizvol'nom razsuzhdenii' dvorianstva v sobytiiakh 1730g." *Problemy istochnikovedeniia,* XI (1963), 237-265.

Puttkamer, Ellinor von. "Einflusse Schwedischen Rechts auf die Reformen Peters des Grossen." *Zeitschrift fur Auslandisches offentliches Recht und Volkerrecht,* XIX (Aug.-Nov. 1958), 368ff.

Riasanovsky, Nicholas V. "The Norman Theory of the Origin of the Russian State." *The Russian Review,* VII (1947), 96-110.

Schlieper, H. C. "Tatishchev's Interest in History." *New Review,* V (1965), 17-24.

Shakhmatov, A. A. "K voprosu o kriticheskom izdanii 'Istorii rossiiskoi' V. N. Tatishcheva." *Dela i dni,* I (1920), 80-95.

Shapot, E. G. "Ankety V. N. Tatishcheva kak istochnik po istorii Sibiri pervoi poloviny XVIIIv." *Problemy istochnikovedeniia,* X (1962), 134-153.

Solov'ev, S. M. "O prodolzhenii istorii Tatishcheva." *Moskvitianin,* X (1845), 164-176.

————. "Pisateli russkoi istorii XVIII veka." *Arkhiv istorikoioridicheskaikh vedenii,* II (1855), first half.

Stepanov, N. N. "V. N. Tatishchev i russkaia etnografiia." *Sovetskaia etnografiia,* I (1951), 149-165.

Tikhomirov, M. N. "V. N. Tatishchev." *Istorik marksist,* VI (1940), 43-56.

Valk, S. N. "Tatishchevskie spiski 'Russkoi pravdy.' " *Materialy po istorii SSSR,* V (1957), 607-657.

Zhelokhovtseva, L. M. "Bibliograficheskaia apravka o V. N. Tatishcheve." *Istorik marksist,* VI (1940), 57-62.

V. UNPUBLISHED MANUSCRIPTS

Cracraft, James. "Feofan Prokopovich." n.d., 49 pages. (Dr. Cracraft is a professor at the University of Illinois at Chicago Circle.)

Feinstein, Stephen C. "V. N. Tatishchev and the Development of the Concept of State Service in Petrine and Post-Petrine Russia." Unpubished Ph.D. dissertation, Department of History, New York University, 1971.

Riasanovsky, Alexander V. "Norman Teory of the Origin of the Russian State." Unpublished Ph.D. dissertation, Department of History, Stanford University, 1960.